THIS OTHER EDEN

David Clarke

Published by Thomas K. Clarke,
Howgill Castle, Milburn, Penrith, Cumbria, England.

The First Edition

ISBN 0-9510385-0-8

Designed by Peter J. Neal, Epwell. Typeset by BEA Typesetters, Banbury. Printed and bound by Ravenprint, Bicester.

TO ELAINE

Preface and Acknowledgements

This is a history of the coming of Methodism into the upper Eden valley, Westmorland. It tells the story of a living religion in a remote, rural area and attempts to understand what it means to belong to such holy communities.

Research has relied considerably on Minute Books, Circuit Plans, Registers, Reports and Letters, to which the County Record Office (at Kendal) has kindly provided most helpful access. Invaluable, too, has been the use of the Methodist Archives in the John Rylands University Library of Manchester. In addition, I am indebted to the Staff of the *Cumberland and Westmorland Herald* weekly newspaper (at the Herald Office, Penrith) who kindly provided me with the facility to read early editions.

John Hall (of Appleby) and Julia Petty (of Staindrop) provided the original photographs and local Methodists (named in the Bibliography) readily gave their assistance. Peter Neal, a Local Preacher in the Kineton Circuit, designed the imaginative cover.

Years ago, my parents — and the fellowship to which we belonged at Catherine Holme — were the inspiration of this project. More recently, my wife Elaine has been my mainstay, especially during my year of study in the Department of Religion at Leicester University. Our children (David, Julian and Joanne) have also added their welcome ecouragement over the years and my brother Thomas kindly made publication possible.

David F. Clarke
Wesley Manse
Kineton
Warwick

May 1985

CONTENTS

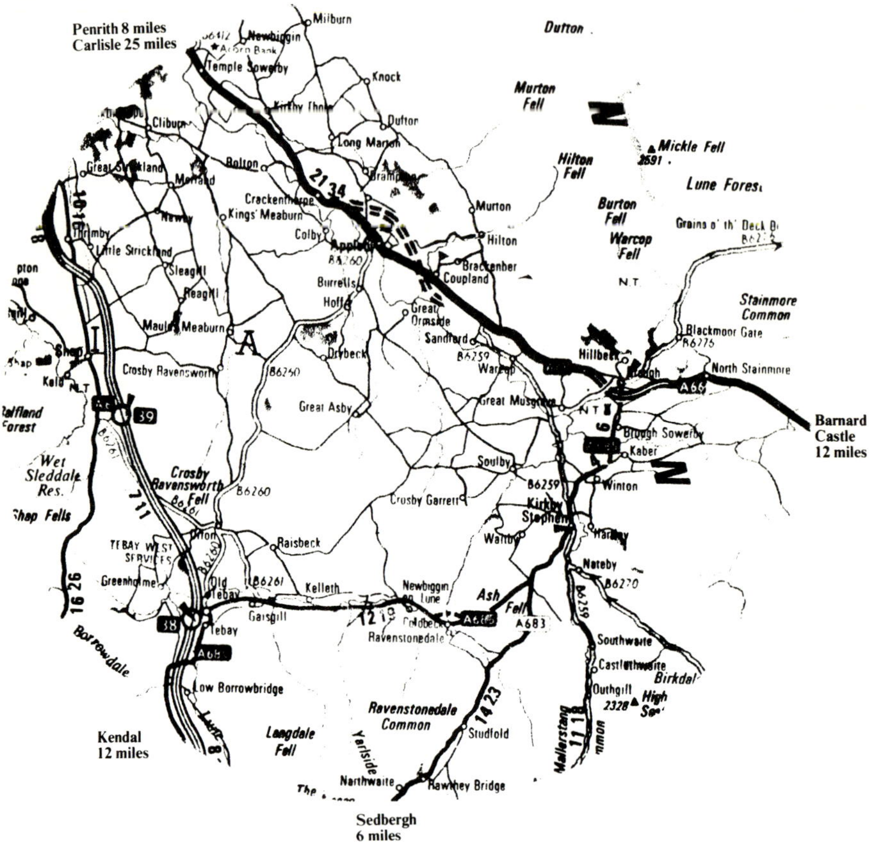

The RIVER EDEN rises about one mile south of High Seat, between Mallerstang Common and Angram Common. It flows north-westerly in general direction, through Kirkby Stephen, Appleby and Carlisle to the Solway Firth.

5 MILES TO THE INCH
Reproduced from the Ordnance Survey Map, Crown Copyright Reserved.

BARNARD CASTLE
WESLEYAN CIRCUIT
MEMBERSHIP FIGURES

	YEARS.										
	1791	1792	1793	1794	1795	1796	1797	1798	1799	1800	1801
	Nos.										
Barnard Castle - -	105	116	108	153	143	102	103	102	99	85	77
Newbiggin - -	30	27	28	39	36	33	33	35	27	27	33
Middleton -	20	18	19	28	21	16	14	13	12	10	9
Egglestone - -	12	11	11	20	15	14	14	13	13	12	..
Cotherstone - -	9	6	4	5	7	10	11	11	12	12	..
Newsham - -	10	9	8	7	7	7	8	8	6	6	6
Barningham - -	6	6	6	7	6	5	6	6	8	5	10
Scargill - -	8	9	9	9	8	7	6	5	7	7	8
Staindrop - -	13	14	10	14	11	12	12	8	9	..	..
Baldersdale - -	8	11	9	6	6	11	12	13	12	9	7
Cockfield and Evenwood	..	14	12	27	22	21	14	15	9	4	..
Lunedale - -	..	..	..	10	10	9	8	..	..	..	—
Bowes	..	..	..	..	..	..	..	..	..	4	7
Bishop Auckland -	..	..	..	..	..	..	..	..	28	30	35
Goodley Hill - -	..	..	..	..	..	..	..	..	..	6	12
Dummy Hill & Temple Sowerby	15	22	..	..	..	7	9	11	12	10	11
Gamblesby - -	41	36	38	36	39	43	40	38	35	40	33
Kirkoswald and Penrith-	7	5	7	6	9	16	10	8	8	8	12
Kirkby Thore - -	..	5	5	13	17	19	20	22	22	19	19
Long Martin - -	13	..	11	13	19	19	16	16	12	14	16
Gaskel Row - -	14	14	12	6	7	..	..	..	..	..	..
Appleby - -	15	10	9	14	14	19	18	18	18	18	20
Winton - -	9	11	10	10	13	10	11	..	..	..	..
Brough - -	10	9	7	13	18	16	15	10	12	10	7
Stainmore - -	..	..	12	20	16	17	14	11	15	13	18
Berryholme - -	..	..	20	..	..	..	..	..	..	..	..
Beathwaite Green -	..	..	..	30	31	..	..	..	..	..	..
Ashby Grange - -	..	..	3	12	7	6	6	7	6	..	..
Cliburn and Morland -	..	..	..	..	40	36	27	24	24	12	11
Longwathby - -	..	..	..	..	..	..	10	..	..	..	..
Renwick - -	—	—	—	—	—	—	—	—	—	—	14
Dufton and Knock -	—	—	—	—	—	—	—	—	—	—	25
Hilton, Bleathorn &c, -	—	—	—	—	—	—	—	—	—	—	13
Kendal - -	20	16	28	45	31	—	—	—	—	—	—
Ravenstonedale -	18	12	14	11	7	—	—	6	—	—	—
Total Numbers......	383	381	400	554	560	455	437	400	406	361	403

Plan of the Wesleyan-Methodist

1

"Hold fast the form o

Places.	Time of Service.			A.	MAY.					JUNE.				
"Meditate on these things."	M.	A.	E.	25	2	9	16	23	30	6	13	20	27	4
Appleby		2		8	11	6	7	9	3	14	12	8q	3	1
Ditto			6½	1	11	2	1	1	2s	2	1	1q	3	2
Dufton		2		9	2	7	1L	8	2	19	1q	6	2s	14
Brough		2		1	8	3	17	1		12	13q	1	9	7
Ditto			7	13	1	3	2	5	1	12	2q	5	1s	7
Kirkby-Stephen ..	9½	2		15	1	12	2	13	1	8	2q	14	1L	[illegible]
Murton	10			1	6	2	11	1	9	2s	8	1q	16	2.
Warcop		2		18	17	2	6	11	9	2qs	19	5	7	2.
Kirkby-Thore ...		2		2	12	1	3	2s	8	1L	7	2q	19	1
Longmarton			7	6	2	11	3	2s	8	1q	7	19	2	11.
Bolton			7	2	12	1	7	11	19	14	16	2q	6	1
Orton	9½	2	7	7	9	4	14	18	11	4	6	3q	12	1
Crosby		2			14		18		17		15q		13	
Peaslands		2		11		8		7		3q		16		6
Knock		2		19		11		6		16q		12		3
Borrowdale		2		-		5		17		10		10q		1
Oxenthwaite		2			15		13		5		10q		10	
Blenkarn		2			19		12		7		17q		8	
Milburn			7		19		12		7		17q		8	
Craikenthorpe ...		2			16		19		6		11q		7	
Soulby		2		3		13		19		7q		17		13
Mallerstang		2		17		18		15		13q		18		1

The Stewards and Local Preachers are requested to publish the Col
The Quarterly Meetings will be held at Kirkby-thore on Wednesday, June the 23rd, and at Appleby on
S Sacrament, L Lovefeast, Q

J. ATKINSON, PRINTER A

...reachers for the Appleby Circuit.

...0.

...nd words." ST. PAUL.

	JULY.		AUGUST.					SEP.				OCT.		
...1	18	25	1	8	15	22	29	5	12	19	26	3	10	17
J	6	9	14	12	1L	3	7	11	14	9q	14	12	8	7
	12	2	2	1	1	3	2	1s	1	2Q	2	1	1	7
	9	2	8	1	3	2	19	1	7	2Q	9	1	14	2s
	1L	5	11	*	12	14	3	9	1	*Q	7	5	1	18
	1	1	11	2	18	1	3	2	17	1Q	7	2s	13	1
	11	1	3	2	15	1	12	2	3	1Q	13	2s	11	1
	1	9	2	19	1	7	2	8	1Q	3	2s	11L	1	19
7	3	*	2L	10	6	7	2	12	8	3Q	2s	14	7	19
J	2	14	1	3	2	6	1	19	2q	12	1s	7	12	3
2	2	14	1L	3	7	2	11	19	2q	12	1s	7	3	2
J	7	11	14	9	2	19	1	6	7q	8	3	9	12	14
4	14	8	7	4	17	11	9	4	6q	18Q	12	4	2s	11
J		7		14		10		13		17Q		3		10
	7		12		11		14		19q		3		6	
	8		19		16		6		11q		9		3	
	13J		5		*		18		13q		5		*	
J		13		5		*		17		13Q		18		*
J		3		11		16		14		7Q		19		9
J		3		11		16		14		7Q		19		9
J		11		9		19		7		8Q		9		14
	10		16		10		15		9q		8		10	
	5		15		13		17		18q		15		13	

Preachers.

'Preach Christ.'

1 L. Heywood
2 W. Jones
3 E. Broster
4 S. Brunskill
5 E. Spencer
6 R. Salkeld
7 J. Dent
8 J. Craig
9 J. Jaques
10 R. Gibson
11 J. Thompson
12 E. Thompson
13 C. Waud
14 J. Stubbs
15 W. Kidd

Exhorters.

16 J. Smith
17 J. Close
18 J. Gowling
19 T. Forest
20 *

...on the preceding Sabbath and make them at the time appointed.
...sday, September the 22nd. The Quarterly Fasts are on Friday, June the 2[illegible]th, and September the 24th.
...y Collection, J July Collection.

...BOOKBINDER, APPLEBY.

Kirkby Stephen and Appleby
WESLEYAN METHODIST CIRCUIT PLAN,
1881-2.

"The Lord loveth the gates of Zion" Psalm lxxxvii. 2

"He that winneth souls is wise." Prov. xi., 30.

PLACES AND TIME.			Oct. 30	Nov. 6	Nov. 13	Nov. 20	Nov. 27	Dec. 4	Dec. 11	Dec. 18	Dec. 25	Jan. 1	Jan. 8	Jan. 15	Jan. 22
KIRKBY STEPHEN ...	Sunday	10½	27C	1	23	2	1	31Q	2	1	33	2	15	21I	2
		6½	45C	1	37	2	W	40Q	25	1	38	2L	19	21I	44
	Tuesday	7		•		1		1		1		1		1	
APPLEBY	Sunday	10½	2	†C	1	40	31	1Q	27	2	45	1	46	9I	32
		6½	13	†C	1	58	31	2Q	49	25	50	1	33	2I	47
	Wednesday	7	2		2		2				2		2		2
BROUGH	Sunday	2	•	55C	38	2	42	44Q	22	60	46	2S	28I	20	18
		6½	•	55C	38	7	42	44Q	30	61	46	52	28I	20	18
	Friday	7						1				1			
ORTON	Sunday	10½	34	9C	53	1	2	55Q	38	47	19	44	23I	1	36
		6½	34	40C	49	31	2	55Q	38	32	27	25	41I	1S	49
	Monday	7					2							1	
GAISGILL	Sunday	2	1	40C	49	19	2S	34Q	25	32	42	25	56I	1	60
		6½	1	9C	53	36	15	34Q	25	47	42	44	56I	10	61
	Tuesday	6½			1				1				1		
HILTON AND MURTON	Sunday	2	46	2S	34C	20	25	47Q	†	52	13	9	45I	22	33
		6½	57	2	34C	20	25	47Q	†	52	13	9	45I	22	33
	Monday	7			2							2			
DUFTON	Sunday	10½						2Q							
		2	58	54	1C	50	49	2SQ	48	33	†	59	13I	55	47
		6½	58	54	6C	50	49		48	39	†	21	13I	55	32
	Tuesday	7			2					2					
LONGMARTON	Sunday	6½	49	26	27C	51	13	21Q	6	33	1S	35	54	4I	39
	Thursday	7			2				2						
KIRKBYTHORE	Sunday	10½									1				
		2	48	47C	51	22	38	59Q	21	55	1S	35	29	2I	13
		6½	6	47C	54	22	38	57Q	21	55		59	29	2I	13
	Wednesday	7				2						2			
MILBURN	Sunday	10½							1		2				
		2	49	50	45C	47	54	57Q		21		26	48	38I	4
		6	31	50	45C	47	54	51Q	1	29	2S	†	58	37I	4
	Wednesday	7						2						2	
BLENCAIRN	Sunday	2	31		13C	6	57	51	4Q	29	2S	†	58I	37	54
		6½	39	26	13C		57		4Q		39		48I		54
	Tuesday	7						2						2	
WARCOP	Sunday	2	53	18	2TC	37	48	•	13Q	31	22	40	27	52I	1
		6½	46	29	2C	37	48	1S	13Q	31	45	40	34	44I	1
	Tuesday	7					1		2		1				2
SOULBY	Sunday	2	27	1	14C	30	41	28	2SQ	49	SS	36	25	19	44I
		6½	42	56	7C	34	41	28	53Q	49	SS	36	38	16	37I
	Wednesday	7					1							1	

PREACHERS

1 T. A. SEED, Kirkby Stephen
2 J. MONAHAN, Appleby
3 E. Thompson, Hartley Castle
4 T. Westmorland, Kirkby Thore
5 T. Fawcett, Kirkby Stephen
6 W. Robinson, Longmarton
7 R. Simpson, Kirkby Stephen
8 W. Fleming, Dufton
9 J. Close, Smardale Hall
10 T. Bousfield, Gaisgill
11 R. Farrer, Orton
12 J. Dinsdale, Bretherdale
13 R. Simpson, Milburn
14 G. Hall, Catherine Holme
15 E. Beck, Gaisgill
16 W. Benson, Crosby Garrett
17 R. Fawcett, Warcop
18 S. Taylor, Soulby
19 G. Handley, Ravenstonedale
20 J. Rudd, Ormside
21 T. Nixon, Milburn
22 J. Pighills, Soulby
23 J. J. Baker, Gaisgill
24 J. Barker, Winton
25 T. Thompson, Maulds Meaburn
26 R. Hall, Milburn
27 W. P. Robertson, Heights, Ormside
28 W. Hall, Warcop
29 E. Williamson, Appleby
30 W. Harrison, Winton
31 T. Moffatt, Orton
32 J. Gowling, Musgrave
33 J. E. Thompson, Hartley Castle
34 T. Whitehead, Kirkby Stephen
35 H. Hodgson, Crosby Ravensworth
36 J. Handley, Gaisgill
37 T. Hall, Soulby
38 R. Sawer, Kirkby Stephen
39 J. Furnass, Knock
40 J. Cooper, Smardale
41 T. Carter, Holme Bottom, Orton
42 T. Capstick, Ravenstonedale
43 R. Braithwaite, Kirkby Stephen
44 R. Balmer, Soulby
J. Lamb, Kirkby Stephen

WAITBY	Sunday Wednesday	6½ 7	z41	19	z40	30	z36	32 1	z16Q	45	z*	55	z42	48	z31 1
KNOCK	Sunday Thursday	2 6½ 7	28 28	21	25C 25C	29 2	53 53	59	15Q 39Q	13	54 54	26	57 57	51	58I 58I 2
ESPLAND HILL	Sunday Thursday	2 6½ 7	14 48	21 39	4C 4C	40 27	† † 2	33 33	54Q 54Q	2S 51	50 58	1 29	46 46 2	9I 38I	57 57
RAVENSTONEDALE ..	Sunday Wednesday	2 6½ 7	33 33	30 30	48C 48C 1	56 55	1 1S	37Q 37Q	23 30	15 19	10 41	32 32	53 53 1	* *	49I 21
MALLERSTANG	Sunday Wednesday	2 6½ 7	38 38	52 52	28C 60C	32 32 1	33 33	19Q 56Q	62 42	44 44	48 48	47 47 1	18 18	30I 30I	7 62
HELM	Sunday	2		30		9		50Q		37		49		40	
ORMSIDE	Sunday	2	2		31		46		41		34		33		29
CATHERINE HOLME ...	Sunday Wednesday	6½ 7	2	36	31C	9	46	50Q	41 2	37	34	49	1S	40I	29
KING'S MEABURN... ...	Sunday Tuesday	2 6½ 7	25	57 57	35C	21 21 2	4	26Q 26Q	6	50 50	29	51 51	2S	31I 31I	35
BRETHERDALE	Sunday	2	A15		D10		L23		A31		D25		L49		D50
CROSBYRAVENSWORTH	Sunday Monday	10½ 2 6½ 7	37 37	44 44	42C 42C	1 1S	45 45	58 58 2	29Q 29Q	35 35	31 31	50 50	2 2 2	27 27	48I 48I
MUSGRAVE	Sunday	6½	20	7	46	44	16	*Q	22	34	28	18	32	52	45
COPELAND BECK	Sunday	2			32				57Q				34		
NATEBY	Sunday Tuesday	2 6½	32 32	60 61	37 28	52 52	18 18	40Q 31Q	42 55	30 30	38 7	16 56	15 44	47 47	2S 53

50 R. J. Todd, Crosby Ravensworth

On Trial

51 J. Richardson, Kirkby Thore
52 C. Bousfield, Brough
53 J. Cherry, Soulby
54 T. E. Etchells, Kirkby Thore
55 T. Braithwaite, Kirkby Stephen
56 W. Nicholson, Kirkby Stephen

Exhorters, &c.

57 W. Nevison, Espland Hill
58 T. Dawson, Espland Hill
59 R. Sinclair, Newbiggin
60 G. Sutherland, Mallerstang
61 G. Brown, Mallerstang
62 Supply
* Kirkby Stephen
† Milburn
W

Circuit Officers.

CIRCUIT STEWARDS:—Mr. J. Close, Smardale Hall, Mr. T. Westmorland, Kirkby Thore.

CIRCUIT TREASURER OF THE WORN-OUT MINISTERS' FUND:—Mr. R. Taylor, Crosby Lodge, Shap; to whom the Contributions from the Classes should be forwarded before Christmas.

NOTES AND EXPLANATIONS

References.

Q—Quarterly Collection
C—Chapel Fund do.
I—Institution do.
T—Tickets
L—Lovefeast
S—Sacrament
SS.—Sunday School Sermons
CA.—Chapel Anniversary

Z—before the figure—Service at Smardale Hall
L— „ „ —Service at Brother Layfield's
D— „ „ —Service at Brother Dinsdale's
A— „ „ —Service at Brother Atkinson's

Notices.

1.—The Quarterly Meeting will be held at Kirkby Stephen, on Thursday, December 22nd; Local Preachers at 10.30 a.m.; Stewards at 1 p.m.

2.—Every Preacher is expected to fulfil his own appointments, or to provide an accredited substitute.

3.—The Society Stewards are requested to give due notice of all the Services, Collections &c., and to forward the connexional Collections to the Superintendent without delay.

4.—The publications of the Wesleyan Book Room may be obtained through the Ministers. Orders should be sent not later than the 17th of each month.

5.—The Wesleyan Chapels at Kirkby Stephen, Appleby, Warcop, and Crosby Ravensworth, are duly Licensed for the Solemnization of Marriages.

6.—The Brethren appointed to King's Meaburn are requested to meet a class after the afternoon Service.

7.—The Copeland Beck Service is now held at Mr. Bellas's, Bank End.

8.—The Conference recommends that, on Sunday December 11th, special reference be made in all our Chapels throughout the Connexion to the subject of Temperance.

PRICE 1½d.

J. WHITEHEAD, PRINTER, APPLEBY.

KIRKBY STEPHEN AND APPLEBY WESLEYAN CIRCUIT PLAN: 1881-1882

SPITAL CHAPEL
(exterior and interior)

Photographs by Julia Petty, Staindrop.

BROUGH SOWERBY CHAPEL
(exterior and interior)

Photographs by John Hall, Appleby.

TEMPERANCE LEAGUE CERTIFICATE: MAY, 1902

CHAPTER 1

Another World

The county of Westmorland which, in 1974, became part of Cumbria, is bounded to its west by the Lake District mountains, to its north by the lower Eden valley, to its east by the Pennine mountains and to its south-east by the mountains of north-west Yorkshire, with the Kent estuary and Morecambe Bay to the south and south-west. The river Eden[1] rises in the east of the county and flows through Kirkby Stephen and Appleby to Carlisle and the Solway Firth. Kirkby Stephen's population was 1,455 in 1971, while that of Appleby was 1,855.[2] The rest of the thin population of the upper Eden valley is found in village, hamlet and farmhouse and is geographically isolated from the rest of Westmorland and from England as a whole.

The county of Westmorland (before turnpike roads and railways) was somewhat gloomily described by Daniel Defoe as a "County eminent only for being the wildest, most barren and frightful of any that I have passed over",[3] but Wordsworth and modern communications have found sunlit valleys and majestic beauty in the mountains. The climate of the Eden valley is less extreme than that of the Lake District but the Pennine Fells can be inhospitable in the winter months. Cross Fell is the highest mountain in the Pennines, being 2,930 feet above sea level, while high ground to the west, south-west and south of the upper Eden valley rises to 1,315 feet on Crosby Ravensworth Fell, 1,619 feet on Grayrigg Common and 2,097 feet on Ravenstonedale Common. The several tributaries of the Eden spring from Mallerstang Common, from the various Fells[4] of the Pennines and from Crosby Ravensworth Fell. These tributaries are often called "becks" or "streams".[5] Mountainous parts are often devoid of trees but lower-lying parts of the Eden valley (e.g. in the Appleby area) have occasional woods (e.g. Hoff Lunn),[6] and copses or plantations. The small villages, hamlets and isolated farms, together with Appleby, Kirkby Stephen, Tebay, Brough and Kirkby Thore, form a thinly-populated area, the scenery, especially down into the Eden valley, in better weather, being green and pleasant. The Eden itself (with a likely Indo-European derivative, meaning simply "water") has an attraction which inspired Wordsworth to address it as "fair Stream!". Even so, the Lake District now draws a larger tourism and when the first Methodists came, in the second half of the eighteenth century, to the upper Eden valley, it was to a geographically remote area. It was to a people who over the centuries, had been subject to Roman, Anglian, Viking, Norman and Scottish invasion and who demonstrated a strong independence in the presence of newcomers, whatever message they had to bring. Geographically, we are dealing with an area of no more than twenty miles (from Cross Fell in the north to Mallerstang Common in the south) by twenty miles (from Crosby Ravensworth in the west to Bowes Moor in the east).

When the Romans came to our particular part of north-west England, some time after 71 AD, they found a Celtic culture and religion to which T. F. Bulmer made reference[7] in his book *History of Westmorland*.

"Caeser inquired the origin of those inhabiting the northern part of the country" and "was informed that they were the spontaneous growth of the soil. They were divided into tribes, the most important of which, both as to numbers and extent of territory, was the Brigantes, who inhabited the district now comprehending the counties of Yorkshire, Durham, Cumberland, Westmorland and Lancashire. They were the most powerful and warlike section of the Ancient Britons, and opposed the progress of the Roman Legions with the most stubborn resistance. They were as wild as the hills amidst which they dwelt, and lived in hovels formed of the trunks of trees, rooted in the earth, and enclosed by interwoven branches.... Of the religion of those ancient Britons our knowledge is necessarily very imperfect. ... Their religious rites were all performed amidst groves of oak, or in deep recesses of the forest. The oak they deemed sacred, and from the monarch of the wood their religion has been called Druidism-Drui, an oak (Celtic)."

Bulmer also said that these Druids sacrificed occasional white heifers, under oak trees, to their gods and living in the deep forest, they also sacrificed, in an open space, fruits of the earth in peacetime and bodies of the enemy during war. The Druids kept all learning to themselves, their precepts being commited to memory by their disciples. They held a knowledge of heavenly bodies which, they believed, influenced the destinies of men. They taught the transmigration of souls and had numerous deities whom they worshipped. Bulmer further described the culture of the Druids: "Every locality had its divinity, and each stream its presiding genius".[8] It took twenty years to prepare for the Priesthood, secrecy "chaining the lips of the initiate". Druids also dispensed justice, helped govern the country and "at their mandate contending armies consented to sheath the sword". Their bards studied poetry and played the harp. Bulmer's picture of these Druids, however, is of a secret, separate group, whose isolated existence we can neither measure nor appreciate. When their Roman occupiers finally withdrew to the Continent in the fifth century, this Celtic culture may even have been renewed for a time. The Romans were followed by Anglian settlement (600-900 AD), though even this visitation may, similarly, not have impressed our particular area a great deal. The later, eight-century Anglian invasion did, however, mean that settlements were established from Stainmore under the eastern fells, down to Winton, Wharton, Hilton, Murton, Dufton and Long Marton.

The Vikings raided and settled in Britain in the ninth and tenth centuries. Their main settlement in the Lake Counties was of Norwegians who sailed and raided southwards from the Outer Hebrides and eastward from Ireland and the Isle of Man. A hill, pastoral people, these Norse made their greatest impact on the cental Lake District, their speech used down to the twelfth century and surviving in modern dialect. In the upper Eden valley, however, their influence was not noticeably felt and culture and religion may even have remained enduringly Celtic; the later Norman Conquest was, however, to have a significant influence, from the eleventh century onwards. For it was the Normans who introduced religious orders, albeit more so into Cumberland than into Westmorland; Shap Abbey (founded in 1119) was the only monastic abbey of any importance in the latter county. In the twelfth century, says Whellan, "there was a great movement in building churches for parishes. Many of the parish churches throughout Cumbria and Westmorland are still entirely or partially Norman."[9] Their impact however was not always to meet man's religious need and although the Reformation introduced some hope, it was the Quakers, the Inghamites and the Methodists (especially), of the seventeenth and eighteenth centuries, who were to bring messages that would satisfy the quest of centuries.

Until such people came, what did many of our people believe and how did they live? Partial enlightenment may be gathered from local nineteenth-century newspapers. *The Cumberland and Westmorland Advertiser incorporating the Penrith and Lake District Chronicle,* for example, refers to Rush Bearing, Witches and Holly Night. Writing about Warcop Rush Bearing held at the Summer Solstice, it recalls opinions on its origins. Villagers, apparently, could recollect how their fathers recalled how an "old maid" used to dance to the Church with rushes on her head. The Rush Bearing was described as being in existence at Warcop from time immemorial. Druidical remains in the area suggest, say the newspaper, that the first Rush Bearings may have coincided "with some great heathen gatherings" but that ancient Christians may then have kept the ceremony which made their churches clean and cheerful but which was once a heathen mid-summer feast, to which were brought fruit, flowers and even bloody sacrifices.[10] Here we may note the use of rushes, or barsom branches, in ancient Indo-Iranian religion: "Few doubt that we have in the barsom ... the 'straw cushion' upon which the gods of the Veda were supposed to sit, as they descended in response to the sacrifice, and upon which also offerings to them were spread."[11]

On the sixteenth of July, 1861, there was a letter in the *Cumberland and Westmorland Advertiser* from an anonymous writer at Appleby, commenting on witches and witchcraft some 60 or 70 years earlier. "The wise fwok"[12] were not numerous in Westmorland but every Parish had at least one: "These witches were malicious and revengeful, especially to any who scoffed at them. If this happened they would read a bad prayer upon people or family or stock and consequent illness or affliction could never be removed, except by another witch. Vegetation and fruit trees could be destroyed. Some witches would change into animals – one had become a hare to attract and then confound puzzled huntsmen. Witch power was often strongest early in the morning, before breakfast. Children doing morning errands were told to avoid those houses where witches lived". As a schoolboy at Tebay, a correspondent in the *Advertiser* (18.11.1862) remembers there were many animated stories about 'Old Mary', the supposed witch. 'Old Mary' was Mary Baines and in further correspondence about her (on January 6th, 1863), a letter from "Castle-Howe-Hill" says she was eccentric, kept cats (though none were black), knitted and also worked for neighbouring farmers during haytime. Occasionally she would witch a churn or addle a nest of goose eggs (if she had not been given butter or eggs).

Holly Night, an annual Brough custom, was related to thanksgiving more than to any fear of evil powers. Thus the *Cumberland and Westmorland Advertiser,* on the twentyfourth of December, 1867, reported (in a news item, signed "W.H.H."):

"The very ancient custom of carrying the holly tree through the town is observed. There are two or three inns in the town which provide for the ceremony alternately though the townspeople lend a hand to prepare the tree to every branch of which a torch composed of greasy rushes is affixed. About eight o'clock in the evening the tree is taken to a convenient part of the town where torches are lighted, the town band accompanying and playing till all is completed. . . . Many of the inhabitants carry lighted flambeaus . . ."

The end of the event seems to have been the carrying of the tree to one of the three rival inns and we are grateful for the positive interpretation which goes on to say:

"Although the origin of this custom is lost and no tradition exists which can be traced, it may not be a strained surmise to derive it from the church ceremonies of that day when branches of trees were carried in procession to decorate the altars in commemoration of the offerings of the Magi. . . In Catholic countries lights and torches always abound in their ceremonies and persons residing in the streets through which they passed testified their zeal and piety by providing flambeaus at their own expense and bringing them lighted to the . . . doors of their houses." No explanation is given why the destination of the tree has been changed from church to inn.

The population of the whole county of Westmorland in 1801 was 40,805 but even the largest centres in the upper Eden valley were no more than 1461 (in 1821) at Appleby and 1141 (in 1801) at Kirkby Stephen.[13] Brough had a population of 694 in 1801 and at Kirkby Thore the total was 783. Warcop's figure was 707, Orton's 1230 and Ravenstonedale's 1138. The figures for the parishes in our area were as below, giving two other counts (1851 and 1971) for comparison.

Name of Parish	*1801*	*1851*	*1971*
Asby	357	412	250
Bolton	324	384	285
Brough	694	773	550
Brough Sowerby	139	117	75

Colby	141 (1821)	147	80
Crackenthorpe	134 (1821)	121	75
Crosby Garrett	177	214	105
Crosby Ravensworth	789	971	475
Dufton	392	488	200
Drybeck	100 (1821)	81	-
Hoff	93 (1821)	93	195
Kaber	135	207	100
Kings Meaburn	178	216	120
Kirkby Thore	783	1104	800
Long Marton	432	726	665
Mallerstang	314	204	70
Milburn	237	320	155
Murton	204 (1821)	212	290
Musgrave	159	175	145
Nateby	108	103	95
Newbiggin	126	114	120
Ormside	171	198	90
Orton	1230	1456	540
Ravenstonedale	1138	939	505
Soulby	237	309	180
Stainmore	530	549	215
Waitby	60	54	50
Warcop	707	740	445
Wharton	80	67	35
Winton	262	257	165

What, then, was the life-style of these scattered communities? A "Literary Antiquarian" suggested in 1827) that our area had a distinctive insularity:

"The manners of an insular people change more slowly than those of Continental nations, and the inhabitants of a mountainous district retain ancient usages longer than the natives of an open country. The latter fact, taken in conjunction with the distance of the north from the centre of politeness.[14] explains the tardy advances of our ancestors in improvement; and the former, relating to the genius of islanders in general, applies with equal propriety to the British nation. In fact, the people of England formerly bore the same inferior relation to Italy, France and the Netherlands, which the natives of Westmorland bore in later times to the inhabitants of the southern counties."[15]

Less seems to be recorded concerning birth than marriage or death. Even so, "the mistresses of families ... met to celebrate the birth of every child; and the expenses of the treat given on the occasion were defrayed by voluntary contributions of the visitors."[16] Marriage was set within confines and the Parish system apparently narrowed the choice of bride. In the eighteenth century, young men who left their villages to seek a bride elsewhere were considered to be social outlaws and sometimes the ladies of a particular village would show their disapproval of those males who 'passed them over' for more attractive partners elsewhere. The ceremony of marriage itself was a festive occasion. The county was divided into LATINGS, so called, apparently, from the North country verb 'to late', meaning to seek or invite, and, attended by the whole lating, each family was summoned to meet on the appointed day by the bridegroom in person. The young of both sexes then accompanied the couple to church on horseback. After the ceremony, a race took place from the church to a venue where, for the rest of the day, time was spent in eating and drinking.

Dying also brought people together. Some evidence of good neighbourliness during times of family bereavement is given to us by our anonymous local historian who says that "when a death happened . . . the heads of houses . . . met to condole with friends of the deceased; and the younger members of the community watched the corpse during the night to the day of interment;" and when a poor person died, funeral charges were alleviated by private donations of the neighbours. The "Literary Antiquarian" continues, speaking[17] of a further custom associated with dying:

"One custom has survived the wreck of many provincial singularities, that shows the high estimation in which wheaten bread was held by our ancestors. It is still considered in many parts of the country in the light of a parting gift or a token of rememberance from the dead to the living; for every person who is invited to a funeral receives a small loaf at the door of the deceased, which he is expected to carry home with him. The antiquity of this present is fully established by the monastic name which it bears; for the people call it by the Latin appellation of Arval Bread, probably from the practice of distributing the loaves in the open air."

This token from the dead to the living is in contrast to earlier times in more distant worlds when the loaf might have been buried with the deceased. The small loaf would be an even more appropriate token if the deceased had been a kind person. Writing of funeral customs at Crosby Garrett, J. W. Nicholson says: ". . . the distribution of 'Arval Bread' had been out of use for some years, but was revived when Anthony Brunskill, senr. died in May 1866. He had expressed a wish that such might take place. The custom of sitting up all night with the dead went into disuse between 1830 and 1840. The nearest relatives sat the last night before the funeral. The bidding to funerals is still kept up at Crosby, but funeral dinners at the inn, are a thing of the past. It is related that four such were provided in 1831, a rather large number for such a small village. Of course, poor people could not bear the cost of the repasts. The first coffin at Crosby to have a name plate upon it was Mr. Wm. Close's who died June 6th, 1836".[18] In more general comment about death, epidemic and custom, Nicholson says: "In the reign of Henry VIII (1538), the compulsory provision of keeping of church registers was ordered. At Crosby, the register for Marriages and Deaths commenced 1539, and Baptisms in 1572. In the reign of Charles II,

Burials were ordered to be made in woollen, with a view to encourage the home industries, and some interments are noted in the register. The plague visited Cumberland and Westmorland severely at different times. In 1623 there was a great mortality in many parishes in these counties, as recorded in the registers, the death-rate being from three to five times the usual average. Crosby Garrett was one of the places which suffered from this terrible epidemic."[19]

Education had come through village school, Church and Grammar School. Nicholson and Burn write: "The inhabitants of this county are generally a sober, social, humane civilised people; owing in some measure to the institution of small schools in almost every village. And in the larger towns, as Appleby, Heversham, Kendal, Bampton, Kirkby Lonsdale and Kirkby Stephen, there are free schools handsomely endowed. Insomuch that it is a rare thing in this county, to find any person who cannot both read and write tolerably well."[20] Lines from Wordsworth's Ecclesiastical Sonnets *(Translation of the Bible)* bear this out:

"And he who guides the plough, or wields the crook,
With understanding spirit now may look
Upon her records, listen to her song,
And sift her laws."[21]

Appleby Grammar School had been in existence before 1453 (as a Chantry School) but was actually founded by Queen Elizabeth I on March 22nd, 1574. A Grammar School at Kirkby Stephen was founded in 1565 by Thomas, Lord Wharton. It was, however, the village school which had provided the basic education, administered long before those self-congratulatory words, anonymously describing the 'peasantry' in Westmorland in the spring of 1867: "No one who has seen these men on a market day or at a sheep-shearing could hesitate to say that they are stronger, more active, more handsome than in most parts of England. Intellectually, too, their rank would be equally high and the standard of education is good. In no country are so small a number proportionately unable to write their names."[22] It was, of course, because of the widespread weekday schools that this claim could be made; indirectly, it was reiterated in an article published at the end of 1867, when it was reported that "Returns from this County in answer to the National Societies' Enquiry into the provisions for Church education have been received from all the parishes and ecclesiastical divisions except one. Five parishes only in the whole county are unprovided with church, national or parochial weekday schools."[23]

Inclination and finance were, as always, factors governing travel. Though gangs of pack-horses were once-, twice-, and sometimes four-times weekly journeys to London with merchandise from Wigan, Whitehaven, Cockermouth, Barnard Castle, Penrith, Settle, York, Ulverston, Hawkshead, Appleby, Cartmel, Milnthorpe, Sedbergh, Kirkby Lonsdale, Orton and Dent BEFORE the opening of the turnpike roads,

Westmorland had always been remote. Manufacturers made their wills and settled their worldly affairs before making long journeys.[24] But post-chaises were introduced in 1754, carriers wagons in 1757, and the first stage coach was seen in Westmorland in 1763. Drawn by six horses, it was called 'The Flying Machine'. It took two nights and three days to make the journey between Kendal and London; an "inside seat" for a youngster cost £3.2s.0d. for the journey. For most people who had to travel, journeys were either slowly on foot, or more quickly on pony or horse; it was not till 1862, with the opening of the Eden valley Railway Line and 1876, with the opening of a new passenger service on the Settle-Carlisle Railway, that the upper Eden began to be less remote. Before then, most Eden people had remained within a few miles of their place of birth throughout their lives. Long before then, however, there were exceptions to this rule — men of families who could be required to do military service, leaving wives and children at home on the farm. Following the distribution of land in Westmorland by William the Conqueror, to various Barons, most of the people of this county came to hold small portions of land. This was because the Barons parcelled out their bigger plots to their inferiors who, in turn, granted portions to several individuals. So that when necessary, the man of the household could leave his family to till while he went to fight — a convenient arrangement in barbaric times. So "every man lives upon his own small tenement, and the practice of accumulating farms hath not yet made any considerable progress ... each man having a portion of land assigned to hime for the Sustenation of the military character."[25]

At the beginning of the eighteenth century in Westmorland, ostentation was almost regarded as a vice and frugality was never thought of as meanness. Richer yeomen wore shoes, at least on Sundays and holidays, but labourers and smaller landholders appeared in church in clogs. The average dwelling was low, small and smoky. The somewhat over-polished style of the "Kendal Chronicle" letters of 1812 turns, albeit in imagination, to the possible way in which winter evenings were spent in these houses. Knitting, spinning of flax and carding wool were necessary tasks and talk "was often disposed to perpetuate the credulity of the times; the favourite topics consisting of apparitions, omens, the mischiefs of witchcraft, and fairy tales ... related by the aged to the young.... In all probability these superstitions came into the island with our Saxon ancestors ... but the freedom of the press encouraged a spirit of enquiry which dispelled the gloom of monkish ignorance and the extension of commerce gave birth to a taste for elegance...."[26] Elegance is, of course, comparative but a local clergyman seemed to confirm that by the middle of the nineteenth century, slow but certain changes had taken place. The Reverend Thomas Clarke, vicar of Ormside, felt able to say, in 1860, that some thousand years earlier "habitations were scarcely as comfortable as modern pigsties, when the inhabitants were coarsely fed and thinly clad, where in place of our food-producing farms lay sterile and unreclaimed moors, vast forests and extensive woodlands."[27]

Farming was the most widespread occupation. It meant employment for various age-groups, the half-yearly "Hirings" providing the labour force. Martinmas hirings at Appleby, for example, in 1864, provided first class men-servants from £10.00, second-class men-servants from £8.00, boys from £4.00, according to age and strength; women-servants from £5.00; and second-class females from £3.10s.0d; girls from £2.00 to £3.00. (These would be rates for six months.)[28] It was at these old, Statute Fairs that long rows of youths standing on the footpath, to be inspected and employed, would wear a wisp of straw in their hats or mouths or upon their dress — to signify employment availability.[29] Farming also meant the gathering together of farmers, on special occasions, to help each other. These were social occasions which were often followed by a meal together. Boon ploughing was a common example, 'boon' being a Scandinavian word meaning a favour, or blessing, or acquisition. Mr G. Nelson, aided by neighbours on eight or nine fallow acres of Drybeck Moor, had his boon ploughing in 1862. He had put on at least 100 cartfuls of good lime and fourteen neighbours turned out to help.[30] That would be at least one representative from each house in Drybeck. The farmer's cart also came in useful in the Ormside parish. Nearly all Reverend Thomas Clarke's parishioners turned out to lead tile from the tile kilns of Messrs. Hill, Bleatarn, to the rectory land at Ormside "where the reverend gentleman (was) making extensive improvements".[31] There was boon ploughing at Great Musgrave three weeks earlier. Mrs Taylor supplied coffee and cakes;[32] interestingly, this occasion saw the guests return home sober. Sheep Clipping was also a social occasion. At Mr. R. Nicholson's farm, "Gilts", Crosby Ravensworth, a united sheep clip, dealing with over 700 sheep, was followed by a good dinner.[33] How far back these gatherings had gone into the nineteenth or late eighteenth century, the local newspaper does not say.

Diversions from everyday work took various forms and some created problems. It took Reverend J. Percival, Principal of Clifton College, Bristol, to open the otherwise undiscussed (yet serious) problem of illegitimacy in the *Times* (24.4.1865) and his long letter was quoted in the *Advertiser* on 2.5.1865 where it could be related to problems which arose from the half-yearly hirings: "Young women should never be allowed to attend evening gatherings of any kind, whether religious or social, except in the company of some elders of the family." Young men, he observed, would enjoy reading but they had nothing to read and there were too few reading rooms with too litte advertisement of too few facilities in them. Indeed, it was Percival's concern that holidays, fairs and hirings were occasions of mischief and he wrote: "I should propose therefore, that all statute hirings be abolished and register offices opened in all towns and that farmers and other employers of servants should be induced, if possible, to put and end to the Whitsuntide and Martinmas holidays and never allow female servants to attend fairs or merry-making except on condition of returning home before dark."[34] A Justice of the Peace was to follow these opinions with further revelations a month later. He wrote to confirm that Cumberland and Westmorland had a larger incidence of illegitimacy than any other Counties in England (proved by the last returns of the Registrar General). He urged that magistrates revise their mode of hearing bastardy cases as young people are often able to be present at the hearing, as members of the public, and enjoy the proceedings with laughter and great interest. He suggested that farmers should require "characters" with the servants whom they will be employing – and that the clergy ought to keep the matter before their people. A Doctor Close preached in Carlisle Cathedral in May 1861[35] on matters relating to these public hirings. He disapproved of the dancing, drinking, revelry and orgies of heathendom which accompanied the festivals. He noted that Magistrates were more tolerant towards drunkards at Christmas and thought that penalties should rather be double for such occasions. Public hirings encouraged immorality and vice and drink, especially among girls. Paths of purity and peace should be encouraged rather than the dances of vice. But as if to say that society was not quite so depraved as some would suggest, an editorial the following week was to say that Whit Monday, once upon a time a great day for bull-baiting, cock-fighting and badger baiting, was now a day on which amusements for the working man were less degrading. National tastes had improved. Museums and art exhibitions were being patronised far more. These were, of course, general comments about the whole country and did not deal with the problems associated with the local Statute Fairs.

Dancing had also become a problem for the Church of England. A correspondent expressed disgust that clergymen had been attending Balls in Penrith. "The pomps and vanities of a wicked world were no place for a holy man of God, and *all* members of the Church, including her Clergymen, ought to renounce Balls and keep far from them."[36] This view was re-iterated two weeks later when a further comment on the same issue said: "The gaity it inspires, the company into which it leads and various evils connected with it render it everywhere unbecoming the Christian who has the utmost need to cultivate seriousness and gravity and to live and act as a pilgrim. ... There is scarcely anything not absolutely and notoriously wicked in which conformity to the world consists more than the amusement of the ballroom."[37]

Before the coming of the Methodists (in the middle of the eighteenth century), what, then, was the impact of religion upon the lives of those who lived in the upper Eden valley? We know that during the reign of Elizabeth I (1558-1603), there were, as Henry L. Widdup suggests,[38] probably about 400 or 500 practising Catholics in the whole of Cumbria, their leader being the energetic John Boste, son of a Dufton landowner. Loyal to his faith and church, he died a martyr in 1594 and was canonised in 1970 by Pope Paul VI. Catholicism was practised secretly and, for another two centuries, even into the nineteenth, it continued it work — sometimes tolerated and sometimes persecuted. In 1861, the Catholic Bishop of Hexham and Newcastle visited St. Catherine's Church in Penrith, when 66 persons were confirmed, of whom as many as 19 were converts to the Catholic faith.[39]

On the other hand, there is little strong evidence to suggest that the Church of England was helping ordinary people in their quest of the sacred. So it was that, at his conversion, Stephen Brunskill, a farmer's son, was to write: "I was born at Gaisgill-Row in the parish of Orton, Westmorland, November 5th, 1748. My parents at this time were members of the Established Church but strangers to experimental religion." He was 26 before he could believe that God loved him and could work in his life, and of the Church of England, he wrote: "I received no benefit. I still remained unconcerned about my soul and a slave to sin."[40]

The Baptists had not, nor ever would settle in any great number, in or near the upper Eden, though there are two interesting newspaper references to Baptisms in the nineteenth century. The first under 'miscellaneous news', is headed "an icy baptism" and took place on the eighteenth of December, 1859: "The ordinance of Baptism was administered to a young lady of Bampton. The spot chosen for the celebration of this rite was a millstream when a large number of people were attracted to the stream to witness the performance of the ceremony."[41] The second rare newspaper reference to Baptists is at Brough, when six ladies received adult Baptism which "was witnessed by many who came to be lookers on."[42]

In the century before the Methodists came, there were also a number of "Seekers", especially in south Westmorland. Small groups of people and scattered across the countryside, they were dissatisfied with the traditional, Christian religion and were seeking to make their own approach to God. They might have been largely unknown to one another had it not been that, through the vitaility, courage and inspiration of one man, they were rallied together. The Seekers were "men of competent Bible knowledge and religious training" and "moreover, of a singularly advanced religious experience . . . they were for the most part young men in the prime of their ardour and strength, who would follow the movings of life rather than the counsels of prudence in shaping the new religious movement to which they had vowed their service."[43] The Seekers were "the product of the religious travail of the age rather than of any one religious sect, and were recruited also from Independents and Anabaptists, and from the Presbyterian and Anglican churches."[44] They "felt the insufficiency of the current doctrinal and external religion," but "were not yet brought into a deeper soul-satisfying experience."[45] "Such persons always appear in epochs of religious unsettlement. . . . As soon as faith in the authority of the church grows faint, and the sufficiency of established forms of rituals is seriously questioned, the primary right of the soul to find God Himself is sure to be asserted."[46] He who rallied these Seekers together was George Fox.

George Fox (1624-1690), a shoemaker from Fenny Drayton (some fifteen miles WSW of Leicester) believed, at the age of nineteen, that he must withdraw from the world. He made himself a leather suit and travelled in a north-westerly direction, via Pendle Hill, on the borders of Lancashire and Yorkshire, to Firbank Fell, some ten miles east of Kendal in Westmorland. Here in 1652, near a great rock known as 'Fox's Pulpit', he delivered a memorable sermon. The rock bears a tablet with the following record:

> "Let you lives speak.
> Here or near this rock George Fox preached to about 1000 Seekers for three hours on Sunday, June 13th, 1652. Great power inspired his message and the meeting proved of great importance in gathering the Society of Friends known as Quakers. Many men and women convinced of the truth on this fell and in other parts of the Northern Counties went through the land and over the seas with the living word of the Lord enduring great hardships and winning multitudes to Christ."

Beginning "as a 'voice' crying in the rural districts",[47] Fox soon became a leader, his conversion having assured him that "God is not above the sky, or at the end of a logical syllogism, but is a living spiritual presence revealed within the soul".[48] Only a converted leather-worker could say "All things were new; and all creation gave another smell unto me than before, beyond what words can utter."[49]

The Quakers became strongest in the SOUTH of Westmorland, chiefly at Preston Patrick, a few miles south of Kendal and not far from Firbank. Two of their local leaders were Francis Howgill (born in 1618) who lived at Todthorne, near Grayrigg, and John Audland (born in 1630) who lived at Crosslands, near Preston Patrick. There was also at Grayrigg (6 miles south-west of Tebay), an Ambrose Rigge, schoolmaster, who became a Quaker. Penrith and Shap were the two most northerly meeting-places between 1654 and 1657; small meetings were held at Great Strickland, Grayrigg, Ravenstonedale and Sedbergh. Appleby, in the upper Eden, had a meeting-place of a different kind: courthouse and gaol combined; a "Justice" could also 'hear' individual Quakers at Kirkby Stephen.

R. S. Ferguson says that the most famous of all early missionaries of Quakerism was George Whitehead (1635-1723) of Orton. "He is, after George Fox, the chief founder of the Society; and, both from the great age he attained and the lead he took in the Society's business, may be deemed, to a great extent, its father."[50] He was born in 1635 (at Sunrigg in Orton Parish). Other local Quakers were John and Alice Alderson, of Ravenstonedale (Alice preached in America, Scotland and Ireland, and died aged eighty-eight, in 1766, at Ravenstonedale), Edward Gay, of Appleby ... Thomas Drewery and George Rooke, of Bolton.[51] The list is further increased as names of those fined between 1650 and 1689 come to light: Edward Winter, of Morland ... John Shearman, of Sleagill ... Thomas and Anne Robinson, of Cliburn ... William and John Barwick, of Shap ... Matthew Dawson, of Hilton, and James Scaife, of Nateby.[52] Land and goods were seized from Quakers, in 1677, in Ravenstonedale, Orton,

Shap, Beetham, Milnthorpe, Heversham, Kendal, Crook and Underbarrow.[53] Goods were also seized from Quakers at Brough, Warcop, Appleby and Bondgate.[54]

The upper Eden valley, however, does not appear to have been much influenced by the Quakers, but, in the middle of the eighteenth century, another religious movement established itself quickly but briefly in our area. It was inspired by Benjamin Ingham (1712-1772), a close friend of John Wesley in the Holy Club at Oxford and on their missionary visit to North America. Like Wesley, he was an ordained Priest of the Church of England but he became more attached to the Moravians, whose headquarters he was instrumental in establishing at Fulneck, Pudsey, near Leeds. Becoming an itinerant preacher, he moved away from the Moravians, being more in sympathy with the evangelical, Calvinist wing of the Church of England and the Countess of Huntingdon's Connexion. He inspired the building of Inghamite chapels in Yorkshire, Lancashire and Westmorland – the last being at Birks (in 1757), which, now closed (as are almost all the rest), is in the Warcop area, some five miles south-east of Appleby. His 'cause' began to disintegrate in 1761, when his authority lapsed, and Birks is now a place for storing animal fodder and agricultural machinery. Obviously, there was here no Wesleyan Methodist (Wesley and Ingham grew far apart), yet the enthusiasm of his preaching, the care of numerous converts and his regard for the Sacraments were antecedents of the more enduring Methodism which was to follow.[55]

John Wesley himself visited Westmorland rarely. His first stay was for one night (3-4 October, 1749) at Old Hutton, about five miles south-east of Kendal, on a journey from Whitehaven to Leeds. (Ingham had visited Westmorland the previous year.)[56] He passed through Ambleside in 1751 and in 1752 he was at Clifton, Penrith, and he visited Kendal in 1753, 1764, 1765, 1767 and 1788. He would have stopped to preach at Appleby on June 30th, 1766, but it was too wet so he went on to Arthur Johnson's near Brough. He visited Appleby again in 1786 (on May 11th), the place which, twenty years earlier, he had described as "a county-town worthy of Ireland, containing at least five-and-twenty houses."[57] He visited Brough again for a cup of tea and a prayer during his second journey through Appleby on May 11th, 1786. It was on his way to Richmond that he preached at a farmer's house, near Brough on June 2nd, 1768,[58] and again on May 10th, 1779, on a journey to Newcastle.[59] Little is said in his Journal about these visits to our area, maybe because there was no marked response. The great eighteenth-century preacher (in commendation rather than condemnation?) could only say that, at Brough, on the second of June, 1768, a little bird sang "without intermission, from the beginning of the service unto the end".[60]

Yet even the coming of a lasting Methodism was to mark an entirely new era. Two documents help to introduce us, at the end of this chapter, to what undoubtedly became expression of those new, personal and cherished religious beliefs which ordinary people began to hold dear. The first of these two documents (belonging to the late Miss M. K. Thompson,[61] a Member of the Long Marton Methodist Church, near Appleby) says, simply:

"This is to certify that we the undersigned being Protestant Dissenters do intend to make use of a House in Long Marton in the County of Westmorland and Diocese of Carlisle (the property of Edmund Thompson) for the religious worship of Almighty God and desire the same to be registered in the Registry of the Consistory Court of Carlisle agreeable to the Act of Parliament in such case directed. John Elliott, Edmund Thompson, James Dalton, Thomas Thompson and Joseph Kearson."

"The above certificate has been registered in the consistory court of the Diocese of Carlisle the twenty eighth day of December in the year of Our Lord one thousand eight hundred and thirteen.

Signed R. and G. G. Mounsey
Deputy Registrars."

The other, a Centenary Book with resolutions and a list of subscribers, dated 1841, also contains sentiments expressing a heartfelt debt to Wesleyan Methodism, and here are thirteen of these testimonies to a new religion, some subscriptions given in memory of deceased relatives and friends:

"Mr. Jonathan Thompson, in memory of a pious grandmother who was one of the first Methodists in Long Marton. £10.10s.

Mr. E. Thompson, junior. £10.10s.

Ann Metcalf, a servant at Brough. 10/6.

A lover of Methodism and a token of gratitude. £1.1s.

A servant. 1/-.

Friend to Wesleyan Methodism. 7/-.

In respect to the person who was instrumental in my conversion. 4/-.

In respect to a Wesleyan Minister, James Bland of Orton. 6d.

For himself, his wife and eight children. £10.

Blacksmith who loves Methodism and would give more if he could spare it. 4/-.

E. Hindson, Rosgill Hall . . . in memory of a dear departed mother who was a Methodist of the right stamp. £1.1s.

A restored backslider. 6d.

Donation from a sister on behalf of a beloved brother who died a short time ago praising God that he ever heard the Methodists. £1."

---

1 See the map facing page 8. Its black circle contains the names of towns, villages and hamlets in the present Kirkby Stephen, Appleby and Tebay Methodist Circuit and defines the approximate area of our study.

2 Census Returns.

3 Daniel Defoe, *A Tour Thro' The Whole Island of Great Britain* (London, 1927), p. 679.

4 Fjall, Old Norse, the local term for hill or mountain.

5 Bekkr, Old Norse (e.g. Drybeck, a stream which sometimes dries up).

6 Lundr, Old Norse, meaning "small wood".

7 T. F. Bulmer, *History of Westmorland* (Manchester, 1885), pp. 14-16.

8 *Ibid.*, p. 16.

9 William Whellan, *History and Topography of Cumberland and Westmorland* (Pontefract, 1860), p. 11.

10 29.6.1861.

11 L. H. Mills and Louis H. Gray, "Barsom", in James Hastings, ed., *Encyclopedia of Religion and Ethics* (Edinburgh, 1909), 11, 424.

[12] The local dialect word for "folk" (or 'people').

[13] Census Returns.

[14] Appleby is 270 miles from London.

[15] A Literary Antquarian, *The Manners and Custom of Westmorland*, and the adjoining parts of Cumberland, Lancashire and Yorkshire, in the former part of the Eighteenth century (Kendal, 1827), pp. 36-37. This, a series of letters, was originally printed in the *Kendal Chronicle* of 1812.

[16] *Ibid.*, pp. 25-26.

[17] *Ibid.*, pp. 22-26.

[18] J. W. Nicholson, *History of Crosby Garrett, Westmorland* (Kirkby Stephen, 1914), p. 97.

[19] *Ibid.*, p. 44.

[20] Joseph Nicholson and Richard Burn, *The History and Antiquities of the Counties of Westmorland and Cumberland* (London, 1777), 1, 9.

[21] William Wordsworth, *The Poetical Works of Wordsworth*, Thomas Hutchinson ed. (O.U.P., 1904), p. 435; this sonnet was composed in 1821.

[22] *Cumberland and Westmorland Advertiser*, 23.4.1867.

[23] *Ibid.*, 31.12.1867.

[24] *The Manners and Customs of Westmorland*, pp. 5-6.

[25] *The History and Antiquities of the Counties of Westmorland and Cumberland*, 1, 9-10.

[26] *The Manners and Customs of Westmorland*, p. 15.

[27] *Cumberland and Westmorland Advertiser*, 7.2.1860.

[28] *Ibid.*, 15.11.1864.

[29] *Ibid.*, 30.12.1879.

[30] *Ibid.*, 16.9.1862.

[31] *Cumberland and Westmorland Advertiser*, 15.5.1866.

[32] *Ibid.*, 24.4.1866.

[33] *Ibid.*, 9.7.1889.

[34] *Cumberland and Westmorland Advertiser*, 2.5.1865.

[35] *Ibid.*, 21.5.1861.

[36] *Ibid.*, 25.1.1859.

[37] *Ibid.*, 8.2.1859.

[38] Henry L. Widdup, *Christianity in Cumbria* (Kendal 1981), p. 71.

[39] *Cumberland and Westmorland Advertiser*, 30.7.1861.

[40] Stephen Brunskill, *The Life of Stephen Brunskill of Orton, 60 years a Wesleyan Methodist Local Preacher, written by himself* (London and Kendal, 1837), p. 5.

[41] *Cumberland and Westmorland Advertiser*, 3.1.1860.

[42] *Ibid.*, 10.4.1866.

[43] W. C. Braithwaite, *The Beginnings of Quakerism* (London, 1871), p. 41.

[44] *Ibid.*, p. 25.

[45] *Ibid.*, p. 26.

[46] Rufus M. Jones, *Studies in Mystical Religion* (London, 1923), p. 452.

[47] George Fox, *The Journal of George Fox*, Norman Penney, ed. (London, 1924), p.x. (From the introduction by Rufus M. Jones).

[48] *Ibid.*, p. xi.

[49] *Ibid.*, p. 17.

[50] R. S. Ferguson, *Early Cumberland and Westmorland Friends* (London, 1871), p. 41.

[51] *Ibid.*, pp. 159-160.

[52] *Ibid.*, p. 199.

[53] *Ibid.*, p. 200.

[54] *Ibid.*, p. 201.

[55] David F. Clarke, Benjamin Ingham (1712-1772), M.Phil. Thesis (Leeds University, 1971). Places Ingham is known to have visited in the upper Eden valley, for preaching were: Appleby, Asby, Burtree, Brackenber, Drybeck, Kirkby Stephen, Ravenstonedale and Roundthwaite, near Tebay.

[56] David F. Clarke, "Another 'Son to Susanna(h)' " in *Proceedings of the Wesley Historical Society* (Chester, December 1972), xxxviii, p. 176.

[57] John Wesley, *The Journal:* Standard Edition (1938), V, 173; Arthur Johnson lived in a "lone house, and there was not time to gather a congregation".

[57] *Ibid.*, V, 276.

[59] *Ibid.*, VI, 234.

[60] *Ibid.*, V, 276.

[61] In 1979.

CHAPTER II

Discovered by the Methodists

The Long Marton Methodists were expressing what many Methodists had already experienced through the preaching of John Wesley. Son of a poor country parson, he was, with his brother Charles, a man who was at ease in "glittering mansions" yet "coldly unresponsive" to anything that rank or wealth might claim.[1] With Oxford University education and Anglican ordination he was well-trained and prepared for his historic calling. "The Puritan's high sense of duty and uprightness of life, the Anglican reverence and esteem for social and institutional religion, the scholar's passion for knowledge, were joined to the fine feelings of a true gentleman who was in the best sense a citizen of the world."[2] His one aim was to spread, beginning with himself, holiness to all the world and he defines this holiness in his Journal in a letter to Lawrence Coughlan:

"I constantly told you . . . it was love; the love of God and our neighbour; the image of God stamped on the heart; the life of God in the soul of man; the mind that was in Christ, enabling us to walk as Christ also walked . . . It is true, farther, that if you love God with 'all your heart', you may 'rejoice evermore'. Nay, it is true still farther, that many serious, humble, sober-minded believers, who do feel the love of God sometimes, and do then rejoice in God their Saviour, cannot be content with this; but pray continually, that He would enable them to love, and 'rejoice in the Lord always'."[3]

For more than half a century he declared this emphasis (1738-1791) and it was to become the experience of a great number of his converts. This experience of the love of God through the individual's faith in Jesus became the discovery which was to revive Christianity in England. Social barriers were crossed and remote places were reached by this 'new' religion. Long Marton Wesleyan Methodists, as we have seen, expressed their gratitude — the more immense when we remember that John Wesley had said of countrymen: "In general, their life is supremely dull; and it is usually unhappy to. For, of all people in the kingdom, they are most discontented; seldom satisfied either with God or man."[4]

We must remember, however, that Wesley worked, strategically, from large centres of population and that often it was his converts who took the message to remoter parts.[5] Thus from London to Long Marton (and beyond) the movement grew, and with it, a set of rules inspired by Wesley's own beliefs. *The Constitutional Practice and Discipline of the Methodist Church*[6] lists these largely unchanged rules, and, however isolated, every Methodist is bound by them. In them, we note, in particular, the reasons for the growth of Methodist Societies, remembering that the rules were for every Member and that they were regardless of social standing or previous religious encounter; they bound the people of Methodism together, in the remote upper Eden valley and the crowded lower Thames, In introducing them, John Wesley writes:

"1. In the latter end of the year 1739, eight or ten persons came to me in London, who appeared to be deeply convinced of sin, and earnestly groaning for redemption. They desired (as did two or three more the next day) that I would spend some time with them in prayer, and advise them how to flee from the wrath to come, which they saw continually hanging over their heads. That we might have more time for this great work, I appointed a day when they might all come together; which, from thenceforth they did every week, viz. on Thursday, in the evening. To these, and as many more as desired to join them (for their number increased daily), I gave those advices from time to time which I judged most needful for them; and we always concluded our meeting with prayer suited for their several necessities.

"2. This was the rise of the UNITED SOCIETY, first in London and then in other places. Such a Society is no other than 'a company of men, having the form, and seeking the power, of godliness; united, in order to pray together, to receive the word of exhortation, and to watch over one another in love, that they may help each other to work out their salvation'."

John and Charles Wesley sign the rules which follow, that is, "Rules of the Society of the People called Methodists" (dated 1743) and we quote the main sections:

"3. That it may the more easily be discerned whether they are indeed working out their own salvation, each Society is divided into smaller companies called Classes, according to their respective places of abode. There are about twelve persons in every Class, one of whom is styled the Leader. It is his business –
(1) To see each person in his Class once a week at least, in order
To inquire how their souls prosper;
To advise, reprove, comfort, or exhort, as occasion may require;
To receive what they are willing to give towards the support of the Gospel.
(2) To meet the Ministers and the Stewards of the Society once a week, in order
To inform the Minister of any that are sick, or of any that walk disorderly, and will not be reproved;
To pay the Stewards what they have received of their several Classes in the week preceding; and
To show their account of what each person has contributed.

"4. There is only one condition required in those who desire admission into these Societies; viz. 'a desire to flee from the wrath to come, to be saved from their sins.' But wherever this is really fixed in the soil it will be shown by its fruits. It is therefore expected of all who continue therein that they should continue to evidence their desire of salvation,
FIRST, By doing no harm . . .

"5. SECONDLY, By doing good . . .

"6. THIRDLY,
By attending upon all the Ordinances of God;
such are:
The public worship of God;
The ministry of the Word, either read or expounded;

The Supper of the Lord;
Family and private prayer;
Searching the Scriptures; and
Fasting or abstinence.

"7. . . If there be any among us who observe them not . . . we will admonish him of the error of his ways: we will bear with him for a season. But then if he repent not, he hath no more place among us."[7]

In a serious attempt to bind Methodists, everywhere, together, to make future plans, and to discuss fundamental doctrine, John Wesley also conducted annual Conferences. His first was in 1744 in London, with "many of our brethren (come from severl parts) who desire nothing but to save their own souls, and those that hear them."[8] There were four lay members and four clergymen of the Church of England, together with the two Wesleys.[9] The second Conference was at Bristol in 1745 when, including the Wesleys, there were three clergymen, six lay assistants and two others.[10] Without a break, until July 1932, the Wesleyan Conference met annually. In the earlier Conferences, at which John Wesley was present, his leadership, enforcing strict discipline, was almost an extension of his Holy Club days at Oxford when the nickname 'Methodist' had been given to his group "by a Fellow of Merton College, in an allusion to an ancient College of Physicians at Rome, who were remarkable for putting their patients under regimen, and were therfore called Methodistoe."[11]

In the course of Wesley's preaching, Circuits were established, that is, groups of Societies. Itinerant or Travelling Preachers, sent by Wesley, visited these various Circuits, some of which contained large numbers of Societies and spread across a wide area. It was an organized, planned Revival. After Wesley's death, the Circuits were grouped into 17 Districts, with three to seven Circuits in each. Each District was allowed to elect one Preacher to the 'Stationing Committee', though, by then, every Preacher knew that he was likely to be moved year by year and that no Preacher, unless there was a remarkable revival, would be permitted to stay in the same Circuit for more than two years.[12] This movement of Travelling Preachers from one part of the country to another must have been an inspiration to remote areas, where new messengers could provide an enchanting link with other lines of advance. The Districts kept Minutes of their meetings (in the early 1800's they seem to have been annual) and the Whitehaven District Minutes (which begin on July 8th, 1801), list Brough as "a Missionary Circuit", together with Whitehaven, Carlisle, Douglas and Peel Circuits.[13] The inter-relationship between Conference, District and Circuit is seen in the same north-westerly District meeting at Douglas in 1805. The question is asked: "Can any improvement be made in this District or any of the Circuits in it?" The answer is given: "We think that an additional Preacher in the Brough Circuit as Missionary will be of very great use as there are thousands of precious souls who have not the Gospel preached unto them nor likely to have it preached unless this be done. A person of respectability and affluence has offered to support Brother Hutchinson for one year and he is willing to undertake it if the Brethren in Conference approve of it."[14]

John Wesley's preachers were told that their text book was the New Testament, though he himself published four volumes of Sermons, appearing in 1746, 1748, 1750 and 1760. These avoided all speculative and difficult doctrine and were concerned only with the experience of Salvation and with Christian ethics. They contained an emphasis on experimental and practical religion.[15] As for the later problem of the Sacraments, local chapel trustees, stewards and leaders could allow the Lord's Supper to take place, but Conference also had to give consent.[16] Wesleyan Travelling Preachers who then administered the Sacraments came to be ordained for that purpose — by the imposition of hands — in 1836.

Though, as we noticed, Brough was in the north-westerly, Whitehaven District in 1804, this was largely a matter of geographical convenience. It had, in fact, been missioned from the east, as was the whole of the upper Eden valley. An enormous Wesleyan Circuit was created in 1757, with Barnard Castle as its centre, called the Dales Circuit. Its task was to organise evangelistic work and establish Methodist Societies in the northern dales. By 1772 it consisted of 32 Societies with a total membership of 1,002, including parts of five northern counties, extending from beyond Hexham in the north to Swaledale in the south and from near Penrith in the west to Darlington in the east. That Wesleyan Circuit was, geographically, half as big again as the present Kirkby Stephen, Appleby and Tebay Circuit of the upper Eden. Prior to this large Circuit being formed, work had already begun at Barnard Castle.

John Bond tells us of the earlier influence of Joseph Cheesebrough, a cobbler from that town. Converted in 1747 at Leeds, he had returned to Barnard Castle about the same time. "His divine instincts taught him to seek the salvation of his fellowmen. A simple tongue touched with the fire of the Holy Ghost was the only instrument he had, but talk, plain unvarnished talk ... with neighbours and fellow-workmen, soon made converts for the Cross. Then, Katherine Graves was fetched from Darlington to help them and she formed a class and established a prayer meeting. No bold evangelist had, as yet, visited the neighbourhood nor public proclamation of the Truth had been made. But the leaven had been cast into the lump and the leavening process was proceeding. It was reported amongst the godless neighbours that a moral wolf had entered their fair valley and it was determined that it should be hunted down. First came mockery and contempt, afterwards came violence. For their greater security an upper room was occupied by the infant Church and God met them there but as they went to and from their Master's garret, troops of human fiends and furies swarmed upon their path. Katherine Graves was pronounced a witch and was pricked with pins in her arms that her mysterious power might exude along with her blood as it is still fancied in

1871 in some parts it will do."[17] A Wesleyan Local Preacher, Anthony Steele, also tells of some of the work at Barnard Castle, before the Dales Circuit was formed. Before 1757, the town was reached by Travelling Preachers and converts from Leeds Methodism and "taken into the Leeds Circuit". As early as 1751 Matthew Lowes, a Travelling Preacher, recalls a "remarkable watchnight we held at Barnard Castle".[18] John Wesley had visited there on February 25th, 1752,[19] but before 1757 "there does not appear to have been any regularly formed Circuit between Leeds and Newcastle". Jacob Rowell was therefore entrusted with the formation of the Dales Circuit which, in 1757, also included Swaledale, Arkengarthdale, Wensleydale, Teesdale, Weardale, Allendale, Alson and Hexhamshire.[20]

A year later, the first Wesleyan Society was begun in the upper Eden valley. "About the year 1758 a society was formed in a small village called Winton, across Stainmore's wintry waste. Richard and Mary Brunskill were among the first members in that dreary part of the Circuit. They were the children of pious Dissenters, and had themselves been brought to an experimental knowledge of God under the ministry of Mr. Ingham and his preachers, during an extensive revival of religion in that part of the country ... Peace and spiritual prosperity did not long continue in Mr. Ingham's society ... Mr. & Mrs. Brunskill amidst this terrible storm stood firm in the faith by which they were saved" ... and ... "gladly opened their doors to entertain" Wesley's Preachers and for "upwards of 40 years, gratuitously and hospitably received them under their roof. Agreeable to this arrangement they were visited by the travelling preachers in the Dales Circuit, once a fortnight. Mr. Rowell's Note Book states that in 1759 and 1760, the number of members in Stainmore was ten, and the quarterly contributions four shilling, to four shillings and sixpence."[21] We may note from this extract that the Winton Society was not formed as a *result* of the Inghamite collapse (which took place in 1761) but that the Methodists disagreed, one suspects, with Inghamite theology.

Stephen Brunskill, who was about ten when Winton Society was formed, reflected in his autobiography on what he thought actually happened among the Inghamites. He believed that they became more strongly Calvinistic and that the two older Brunskills "could not, as many had done, call all that ... they ... had heard and experienced ... (of) ... the loving kindness of the Lord a delusion but continued to believe and steadfastly to maintain that Christ tasted death for every man. For these reasons the ... (Inghamite) ... preachers refused to come to" the Brunskill house. The Brunskills, therefore, made "application to the Preachers in connexion with the Reverend John Wesley but the former professors of religion had rendered themselves so odious to the ungodly by their contentions and loose morals that scarcely any would come to hear. Attempts were made at different times both by travelling and local preachers for about ten years before they saw any fruit of their labour. It was indeed with difficutly that we got preaching at all as the nearest Society Mr. Wesley had was twelve or fourteen miles distant."[22] The Winton Society may only have had Richard and Mary Brunskill at the beginning, as its Members; the ten Members in Stainsmore are not listed as a Society in the Dales Circuit in 1760 but in the Circuit Book of 1768, both Winton and Stainmore appear as Societies. But for persistent visiting by Dales' Preachers, this precarious foothold to the west of the Pennines in Winton might have come to nothing. Here was one isolated family which a wider Methodism had rescued, in line with other Eden villages in the path of conquest.

In the Barnard Castle area (only 10 miles east of the Westmorland border), preaching continued fervently in the 1760's. Joseph Benson, from Melmerby in Cumberland, for example, had become a Wesleyan Travelling Preacher in about 1765 and Steele recalls his style of preaching (on the text Daniel 5, verse 27: "Thou art weighed in the balances . . ."): "As he proceeded in the course of his sermon to weigh different characters, as they presented themselves to his glowing imagination, when he came to the covetous man, with all the energy of his soul, and at the top of his peculiarly shrill voice, he cried aloud 'Help! men and brethren help! He is so fast glued to the world, I cannot get him into the scale.' The effect was electrical, and those who heard never forgot it."[23] Was it this new eccentricity of delivery (echoing some of the earlier Quakers), or the sheer weight of theological content which caused open-air preaching to be interrupted and eggs to be thrown? Whichever it was, the Dales Circuit Book of 1768 shows that, in addition to Winton and Stainmoor, the names of Alston, "Melerby",[24] Richmond, Reeth, Darlington and Bishop Auckland were also included.[25] Steele quotes a Mr. Hunter, also appointed to the Dales Circuit (in 1771), who described the spread of the Wesleyan work: " 'We had such a work of God in several parts of this circuit as I never saw. Hardly anything of the kind hath exceeded it in England, both with regard to its swiftness and depth; the power of God bore down all before it, and it seemed as if God was about to convert all the world.' "[26] Wesley himself said of it that "we may affirm such a work of God as this has not been seen before in the three kingdoms."[27] By 1772, Stainmore had 15 members, Soulby had 19, and Long Martin had been added, with 7.[28] The Revivial was spreading westwards, though not yet with the same remarkable success as in the area of Barnard Castle and Weardale. Of the 46 visits which John Wesley made to the North East of England, his impression left at Barnard Castle was profound. "No wonder that the society in Barnard Castle deeply participated in the general mourning which was manifested at the loss of such a father in Israel, especially when it is taken into account, that for nearly 40 years, he had periodically visited the place, and entertained a cordial attachment to the people."[29]

The conquest of the upper Eden appears less spectacular, but when Barnard Castle became a separate Circuit from the Dales Circuit in 1791, its Membership statistics[30] show that the advance had begun and that, for example, Long Martin's membership had increased to 13, a society at

Appleby had 15 members, Winton had 9, Brough had been added with 10 and Ravenstonedale with 18. The next 10 years saw Kirkby Thore, Ashby Grange[31] and Goodley Hill,[32] Dufton and Knock, and Hilton and Bleatarn added to the extensive Circuit. In 1803, Long Martin's name was heard in Conference. "At the Conference of this year Mr. Thomas Graham, a young man from the west side of the circuit, was called out into the ministry. He was a member of the Society at Long Martin, near Appleby, and had been employed in his own neighbourhood as a local preacher for about six years."[33] In the same year, at Conference, Brough was constituted the head of a circuit, "including Penrith, Gamblesby and its neighbourhood, together with all the societies in Westmorland which had previously belonged to Barnard Castle circuit. By this division, two hundred and thirteen members were transferred to Brough leaving two hundred and ten to Barnard Castle. The step was no doubt judicious, the round previously being too extensive, not only requiring the maintenance of a horse, but involving a heavy tax on the physical powers of the preachers, some of whom were advanced in years, and unable to cope with lengthened journies, over wild barren moors."[34] By 1812, Brough Circuit Membership had increased to 273[35] and in 1818, Long Martin, Bolton and Murton were to have chapels.[36] Chapels were also to be built at Dufton and Kirkby Stephen in 1820[37] and at Warcop in 1821.[38] At the 1823 District meeting, Appleby was to have a chapel and had "promised to raise two third of the expense before they commence."[39] In 1824, the District recommended that Brough and Penrith Circuit be divided;[40] this was strongly urged the following year, "Appleby to be the head of the old one."[41] Appleby became a separate Circuit in 1825 and, three years later, John Crosby, aged 23, offered himself, from it, as a Travelling Preacher. The District Meeting confirmed in the necessary Connexional procedure, that "His character is unblemished. He is truly devoted to God. His health is good. He has no matrimonial engagement. He has good preaching talents. He passed the Quarterly Meeting[42] unanimously and his examination was creditable to himself and very satisfactory to the brethren at the District Meeting."[43] John Crosby died of the Typhoid Fever in the Kendal Circuit, aged 27.[44] By 1830, as the Plan on page 10 shows,[45] Orton, Crosby, Peaslands (Kings Meaburn area), Oxenthwaite (4 miles ENE of Winton), Blenkarn, Milburn, Craikenthorpe and Mallerstang were all new Societies; Orton had a chapel built in 1833. The word "Plan" suggests a missionary strategy, the "Preachers" being local and the "Exhorters" being, as Wesley intended, "helpful when there was no preacher in their own or the neighbouring societies, provided they would take no step without the advice of those who had more experience than themselves."[46] His letter to James Barry (on June 24th, 1776), a Travelling Preacher at Barnard Castle, says: "Fix a regular plan for the local preachers, and see that they keep it. You cannot be too exact in this and every other part of discipline.[47]

The District Meeting at Penrith, on June 4th, 1839, approved the building of chapels at Kirkby Stephen and Ravenstonedale. In 1840, Blencarn was to have a Chapel and Knock to have a building purchased and converted into a Chapel, subject to the June Quarterly Meeting's approval and other Connexional requirements being satisfied,[48] and Gaisgill was recommended to have a Chapel at the District Meeting of May 18th, 1841. In 1842, the Appleby Circuit Membership was 404 and there were 12 Sunday Schools, two libraries, 83 teachers and 537 scholars throughout the Circuit.[49] In 1844, of the 3,525 Members in the whole District (the Circuits being Carlisle, Brampton, Whitehaven, Workington, Penrith and Penruddock, Wigton and Keswick, Kendal, Ulverstone and Dumfries), Appleby's Circuit total had increased to 427, only Kendal, Penrith and Workington having higher memberships.[50] Work among young people continued in Sunday Schools but when, in May 1853, the usual District Meeting question was asked "Has the religious oversight of the young especially by the formation of catechumen classes been duly attended to?" the answer given was: "An oversight has been taken of the young but there are many difficulties in this District to the formation of catachumen classes." Whatever these difficulties were, the Sunday Schools, though not the only hope, were a likely environment from which members could be received. In 1864, District membership was 3,857, of whom 462 were in the Appleby Circuit. In 1867 a chapel was built at Espland Hill (between Appleby and Long Marton) and, as at other District meetings, it was notified that the Circuits were giving to the Worn Out Ministers Fund, the Theological Institution (the first being at Didsbury, opened in 1842), Kingswood School and Chapel and Education Funds. This was in keeping with the spirit of Wesleyan Methodism and an indication that each society did *not* exist in complete isolation. The significance of these funds, however, could not have been easily regarded as locally relevant, even though Wesley had written to James Barry, in 1776, "If they now collect only for themselves, how does this help me to carry on the general work?"[51] In theory, a District Meeting should have made the various Funds relevant, but how could a couple of dozen representatives dispel the view that a Wesleyan school or college, a chapel at the other end of the country, or a weary Minister, were not necessarily part of on-going local work?

District permission was given to build a Chapel at Knock in 1873 and in 1874 the District Minutes showed that Appleby Circuit's Membership of 553 was, apart from Ulverston's (with 652), the highest in the District total of 4,993; also, Warcop had a chapel in 1874 and in 1875 a William Denny of the Appleby Circuit offered for the Ministry. He had been, at the age of 22½ years, a hired local preacher in several Circuits and a report on his trial Service was full of hope:

"The reading of the Scriptures was solemn and impressive but spoilt by a perpetual forgetfulness of the existence of the letter 'h'. His voice is good, his action excessive, his earnestness unmistakable as vehement exhortation formed the bulk of the Sermon. Still with all these defects there appeared to be plenty of good raw material which by the discipline of the Institution would develop into a useful preacher of the Gospel. If he can have that discipline we recommend him as a candidate for our Ministry."[52]

In the usual great variety of business, the District Meeting of 1875 also recommended Crosby Ravensworth to build a Chapel (at a cost of £446). In 1878, Mallerstang was to have a new Chapel at a cost of £155. In 1879 (at a September District Finance Committee) agreement was given for the erection of Catherine Holme Chapel (between Ormside and Great Asby). The Chapel was opened 15 days later! The 1880 District Meeting heard that Catherine Holme's case "could not be delayed without the loss of valuable and important help in the erection. The Superintendent (was) in communication with the Chapel Committee." The Appleby Circuit was renamed the Kirkby Stephen Circuit in the 1879 District Minutes and its membership was listed as 620. In 1883, Crosby Garrett chapel had been "begun without consent". In 1885, Thomas S. Braithwaite, a clerk with good health, offered for the Ministry. Jospeh Birkbeck and Peter Thompson offered in 1886. By 1891, the District was to make a contemporary comment on what Wesleyan Methodism had become. The movement had begun when Wesley had stressed the supreme important of holiness, yet when, in a letter from the President (in April, 1891), the possibility of recommending Social Purity Societies was suggested, the Whitehaven District Meeting (of May 12th, 1891) could only withold its support, saying: "Our organisations are already so numerous and complex."

Soulby Chapel was erected in 1892 for £512. In 1893, the District Meeting was called a District Synod for the first time in the District Minutes. At this gathering, there was an awareness of more than belonging only to "complex organizations". In a report on District Evangelistic Work, "Mr. Weston, the District Lay Agent, (had) conducted a fortnight's mission at Kirkby Stephen which was remarkably successful. Over 30 persons of varying ages professed to have obtained a change of heart while a considerable quickening of the Church (had) resulted in improved attendance at the Class Meetings and other Services." From the 1898 Synod we learn, also encouragingly, that in most of the Circuits, Theological Classes or Libraries existed to assist the Local Preachers. At the turn of the century, the 1900 District Synod was presented with an array of figures to convince — if there should be any doubt — that the 1758 Society of Winton ("across Stainmore's wintry waste") had now become part of a vast, administrative unit in which the implications of 'experimental' religion were clearly seen:

Membership	6,749
Members in Bible Classes	385
Wesley Guilds	17
Mutual Improvement Societies	5
Class Leaders	411
Sunday Schools	196

Scholars	15,589
Day Schools	2
Bands of Hope	123
Members of Bands of Hope	9,888
Temperance Societies	31
Members of Temperance Societies	1,355
Fully Accredited Local Preachers	490
Local Preachers 'On Trial'	49

A year later Robert Hutchinson from the Kirkby Stephen Circuit, a 24½-year-old farmer, was approved entirely by both Quarterly Meeting and Synod as a candidate for the Ministry. At the same meeting, Local Preachers were to be requested to join the Connexional Union for Biblical and Homiletical Study and all Local Preachers On Trial were to be urged to take the Classes specially arranged for their benefit. In 1909 a successful mission at Knock was reported; under the preaching of a Circuit Missionary "more than 20 were brought to decision for Christ." In 1910, Milburn applied to have a new Chapel. In 1913, Mr. Norwell's February mission at Appleby attracted several young people and the formation of two new Society Classes. This Lay Evangelist had conducted 4 Missions; but stormy weather, a severe epidemic of measles, and other adversities prevented him from seeing the full fruit of his labours. In 1914, the District Membership was 7,372, of whom 919 were in the Kirkby Stephen Circuit and, after six eventful years, in 1920, while the District Membership was reduced to 7,033, that of the upper Eden Circuit was down, tragically to 621.

Some Circuit Plans in the County Archives at Kendal add further details to the history of the growth of local Wesleyan Methodism. The Kirkby Stephen and Appleby Wesleyan Plans, in the early 1880's, for example, include Bleatarn, Waitby, Helm, Ormside, Musgrave, Copeland Beck and Nateby, making a total of 29 Preaching Places. A note (No. 8) on the January-April 1882 Plan shows visiting 'special' preachers from Newcastle, Liverpool, Headingley, Sunderland and London. A year later preachers are Planned to come from Chester, Birmingham and Newcastle-under-Lyme. Such visiting preachers come rarely but help overcome local isolation from more distant Methodism. The 1901-02 Plan is called the Kirkby Stephen, Appleby and Sedbergh Circuit and has 40 Preaching Places on it, including a footnote to say that "the Conference directs that public collections be made ... in all our chapels ... for the Twentieth Century fund." The purpose of this was to raise enough money to ensure that there would be a Wesleyan Chapel in every village and hamlet in the land. The Kirkby Stephen and Appleby Plan of 1920 has 31 Preaching Places, including Bretherdale, Waitby and Drybeck. These are omitted from the 1929 Plan which thus has 28 Places. A series of accompanying letters and signs signify special events or collections and, on various Plans, samples of these are as follows:

1901 (April-July)

"*T* = Renewal of Tickets

W = Worn-out Ministers' and Widows' Collection
E = Education Fund Collection
K = Schools Fund Collection
CM = Camp Meeting"

1901-02

"H = Horse Hire Fund Collection
† = Circuit Conveyance and Driver
* = Go with conveyance
B = Circuit Bicycle
CS = Covenant Service
I = Theological Institute Fund"

1902-03

"FL = Fire and Light Collection
T = Trust and Quarter Board Deficiency
Supply = Preacher to be obtained"

1929(January-March)

"FS = Flower Service
CH = Choir Services
TS = Trial Sermon"

1929 (April-June)

"YP = Young People's Service
OA = Open Air Service"

Whatever the strength of Wesleyan Methodism in 1932,[53] we can be certain that the intention was the same as it ever had been and that Preachers, Class Leaders, Trustees, Congregations, Ministers and Superintendents were all part of a movement determined to succeed. Worship was repeated, Sunday by Sunday. Beliefs were stressed and re-stressed in Preaching and at the issue of the quarterly Membership Ticket, and the identity, though about to receive a new dimension in 1932, was beyond question. In all this, it became apparent, as we shall see in the next chapter, that people who lived in faraway countries were sometimes dearer to the hearts of our local Methodists than were those who lived in the cities of their own country. A plaque, such as there is in Trinity Methodist Church, Barnard Castle, to the memory of Reverend George Brown (born in that town in 1835) speaks of him as having been "A Renowned Missionary, an ardent explorer, a learned scientist. Most of his life was spent in the South Sea Islands, where he was instrumental in God's hands in the conversion of multitudes of native savages from cannibalism to Christianity." Given he was a native of Barnard Castle, and thus, probably, with honour in his own country, we nevertheless wonder if the same praiseworthy tribute would have been erected had his work been confined to the "multitudes of natives" in cities of his own country.

In 1932, there were 2,510 Wesleyan Methodist Ministers in Great Britain, 18,785 Preachers, 517,551 Church Members, 6,952 Sunday Schools, 115,624 Officers and Teachers, 770,716 Scholars and 8,152 Churches with seating accommodation for 2,339,771. But also, in 1932, among the Primitive

Methodists, there were 1,131 Ministers, 12,896 Local Preachers, 222,021 Church Members, 4,006 Sunday Schools, 52,457 Officers and Teachers, 377,792 Scholars and 4,356 Churches.[54] Indeed, in the Primitivie Methodist Circuit, overlapping the Wesleyans in the upper Eden, there was in 1932 a Membership of 417[55] in 14 Societies, the Wesleyan Membership, at that time, being 727 in 26 Societies.[56] We must now examine, therefore, how it was that a parallel movement had come into being and to what extent, locally, the nature of its principles and aims were the same or different from those which belonged to the Wesleyans – whom it ultimately joined.

Two early nineteenth-century Wesleyan Methodists, Hugh Bourne and William Clowes, became unwelcome in their Staffordshire (Burslem) Circuit because of their enchantment with open-air preaching and American Camp meetings. But Wesleyan response to this kind of activity was reflected in its Minutes which Cyril J. Davey quotes:

"'What is the judgement of the Conference concerning what are called Camp Meetings?' 'It is our judgement that even supposing such meetings to be allowable in America they are highly improper in England and likely to be productive of considerable mischief, and we disclaim all connexion with them.' "[57]

Since both Bourne and Clowes became sympathetic to less spectacular adaptations of this kind of open-air evangelism, their Wesleyan Circuit had no option but to expel them. Thus, in 1811, Primitive Methodism began when eight groups, or Societies, of like-minded approach to evangelism, elected James Steel their first circuit steward and set apart Crawfoot and Clowes as Preachers among about 200 members. Bourne, who was to shape the movement, was "moulded amid the silence and seclusion of the uplands. Bleak, desolate, lonely, and no road, public or private, not even a footroad to it or anywhere near it, Fordhays Farm, in the Parish of Stoke-upon-Trent, Staffordshire,"[58] was his place of origin. The description might be that of Firbank Fell and we note that in the early part of 1799 Bourne had read the books of the first Quakers which, with a printed sermon by John Wesley and "Letters on the Spiritual Manifestation of the Son of God" by John Fletcher, were instrumental in his conversion. James Crawfoot, the first Primitive Methodist Travelling Preacher, had considerable stature as an orator and lived in retirement in Delamere Forest, Cheshire. "The singular effects produced by this man's preaching were by some ascribed to the possession of miraculous powers; by others, to the exercise of the black arts ... His vivid realization of the spiritual world, invested his prayers with an intimacy with the Almighty which gave the impression to those listening to his wonderful voice as he prayed that he actually saw the Lord with bodily eyes."[59] The succession of these travelling Preachers, however, had not intended to be schismatics nor constitutional reformers, but evangelists who wanted to return to the Primitive spirit of Wesley's early conversion days. Even so, they built chapels and their greatest opportunity was often among industrial and agricultural workers; later on, Trade Unionists emerged from their ranks,

Joseph Arch being a Local Preacher who, on February 14th, 1872, lent his personality, leadership and eloquence to the cause of a Farm Worker's Union at Wellesbourne, in south Warwickshire.

The first Primitive Methodist Annual Conference was held in 1820 when it was decided that Circuit representatives should be two laymen for every Travelling Preacher, a distinguishing feature of the movement. Procedures of evangelism were laid down by agreeing that either a town would apply for a Preacher who would then gather together a Society, or a town or Circuit would decide to send preachers to 'mission' hitherto untouched areas. The Hull Primitive Methodist Circuit became a vast collection of Societies formed by the latter method. Clowes went on a Preaching tour in the 1820's through North-east Lincolnshire, Yorkshire, Durham and Northumberland. From Northumberland he crossed England to Cumberland and Westmorland. In 1819 there were four Circuits in Primitive Methodism; in 1824 there were 72 (in four Districts). The membership of the Connexion had risen in five years from 7,842 to 33,507. By 1842, when Bourne and Clowes had handed the work over to others, the total was 85,000. A measure of its progress, nationwide, was reflected in its membership total of 132,000 in 1860.

Its Conferences were numerically small and made up of senior men; Districts were more important than the Connexion as a whole. Stationing of preachers was by and within Districts and in this there was a distinct difference from the Wesleyans who, appointed by Conference, would travel more widely and bring the experience of work in places far separated from each other. By the 1870's, however, Primitive Methodist Districts were made smaller and the Conference was enlarged; Ministers then came to be appointed over much wider areas. A Theological Institute was opened in Sunderland in 1868 and in 1901 the words 'Primitive Methodist Church' took the place of 'Primitive Methodist Connexion'. Before then (and since) "Rules and Regulations for the Societies of the Primitive Methodist Connexion", from the Conference Minutes (1838) show many similarities with John Wesley's rules of 1743. For example,

"1. Q. Who compose the Primitive Methodist Connexion, and what are its arrangements?

A. The Primitive Methodist Connexion is composed of Protestant Christians, united for mutual assistance, in working out their own salvation, and extending the kingdom of Christ. And it is arranged in societies, circuits and districts; and the societies are formed in small companies, called classes; one member of each is styled "The Leader", and usually another, the assistant leader. The CLASSES meet weekly. The members of each have their names on a class-paper, and each member holds a society ticket. The tickets are renewed quarterly at which time a visitation of the classes takes place."[60]

In the early autumn of 1821, Samuel Laister and William Evans went to Barnard Castle as Primitive Methodist Preachers and a Society of 9 people were formed. When William Clowes went there the following February, he found 120 members. Barnard Castle then became a base for extensive missionary effort. William Summerside was sent to Superintend the Circuit in 1828 when a chapel was built. The Branch then included Middleton-in-Teesdale, Kendal, Brough and Penrith. "There were four preachers in the Station in 1836 and in order to go their rounds it took each six weeks away from headquarters. They seldom saw each other, except at the Quarterly Meeting, to reach which a journey of 20 to 40 miles had to be taken on foot."[61] Hugh Bourne visited Brough in 1831 and afterwards went to Mouthlock, 4 miles away, to preach in the new chapel. At that time Camp Meetings were being held outside town and village, one on Dufton Pike.[62] "The entrance of Thomas Batty into Brough in the autumn of 1823 made a commotion. He commenced his campaign in the open-air of course. A horse-block, in front of a public house, was his pulpit, permission for the use of which had been granted to him by the landlady. There was a considerable assembly, the bell-men had been about, and at the close of his sermon he informed his hearers that he was a PRIMITIVE Methodist Missionary and announced his object in visiting the place. A friendly woman at Brough Sowerby, a village about a mile away, entertained him for the night. His kind hostess was soon afterwards brought to God and a Society was established at her place of residence. A chapel stands in the village now."[63] As with the Wesleyans, there were times of remarkable revival. In the spring of 1850 "there was a great spiritual upheaval throughout the whole county and it is estimated that 400 souls were added to the various sections of the church of Christ in Westmorland at that time."[64] There was another such revival in 1863-1864. Before 1886, the Brough Primitives were part of the Sunderland District, but, in 1886, they became part of the Carlisle and Whitehaven District which, as with Wesleyan Methodists, meant that their connexion with the pioneer evangelists from the east was broken in favour of a more suitable geographical unit. This was, in fact, to intensify the isolation which already belonged to the upper Eden which, in distance, was far from Carlisle and Whitehaven; which, by altitude, was separate from the eastern side of the Pennines, and which, in fellowship, was less bound to those in the north-west who had little to do with the new religious movement of our area.

It would be difficult to prove that Primitive Methodism became rooted in the upper Eden because of any widespread dissatisfaction with Wesleyan Methodism. On the contrary, there were numerous instances of sympathetic understanding between these two branches of Methodism who were in the work of evangelism together: in which they were separated from, and undoubtedly more determined than, the local Anglican Parishes. When Batty came to Brough in the 1820's and experienced crowd harassment, it was Mr. Langmire, a Wesleyan draper, who stood firmly by him, promising finance if necessary – and he was as good as his word. In the obituary of the Primitive Methodist, Emma Laverack of Brough, we note the Wesleyan influence: "She remained for years a stranger to the saving influence of divine grace and was first brought under conviction for sin by the labours of the Wesleyan Methodists from whose efforts she also derived some spiritual comfort."[65] In a Memoir of John Bland, a native of Brough, we find he moved with his parents to Burley in Yorkshire and "was brought under the Wesleyan Ministry and became a new creature in Christ. His removal to Leeds brought him into connection with our people and their style of preaching and their incessant labours won his affections and he united with them in Church fellowship."[66] Isaac Johnson, a Primitive Methodist who died at School Hosue, in the Brough Circuit, on September 2nd, 1860, had joined "the Wesleyans and continued with them for about 20 years", some 30 years before his death.[67] Henry Allinson, born on March 15th, 1800, at Couldron Snout in Birkdale, Westmorland, had listened, with profit to Wesleyan Local Preachers when he moved to Lunedale in Yorkshire in 1818.[68] Ann Jackson who died on March 26th, 1848, at Tebay, was a Wesleyan from her conversion to the age of 32 when she was married to a Primitive Methodist and "he being a member of our denomination and having preaching services and Class meetings in his house, she seemed providentially called to unite with him in the support and spread of our sectional interests. Still she loved the people with whom she was united in Church fellowship and left them not from offence, but conviction of duty. She deemed her denominational change as a removal from one branch of the same Methodistic family to that of another and both branches shared largely of her love and prayers."[69] Her funeral was in the Wesleyan Chapel at Gaysgill, "kindly lent us for the Service."

The Hull Primitive Methodist Circuit operated north of an imaginary line stretching across the country from the Humber to the mouth of the Ribble and it was formed in 1819.[70] In its Barnard Castle Branch, by early 1831, Societies included Brough Sowerby (14 members), Brough (30), Ravenstonedale (8), Dufton (12), Long Marton (1), Mouthlock (11), Bleatarn (4), Ormside Mission (2) and Sandford (6).[71] Eight years later (in 1839), the whole Hull Circuit had a membership of 1,556. Barnard Castle became a separate Circuit in 1840 and, to continue the control of a wide expansion, Brough became a separate Circuit in 1849 — with William Fulton as its first Superintendent. There was a Sunday School at the Brough Society in 1841[72] and Mouthlock had one in 1843. In 1844, along with the usual statistics, there was an unexpected documentation of Primitive humanity, at the Barnard Castle Circuit Meeting. A "popular Local Preacher and Leader got basely and publicly drunk. Another Leader, an aged man, then seriously injured the cause by a courting affair. Also a Travelling Preacher who had stood high in this Circuit came from his Station, married one of our Members as privately as possible, sat down upon us, entered into business and was presented by his wife with a son five months after their wedding day."[73] Both Primitive and Wesleyan Travelling Preachers were required to have high standards and these Circuit Reports show such discipline as well as more statistics. Miles Moss (a Travelling Preacher in the Kendal Mission — also part of the Barnard Castle Circuit) was described as "attentive to discipline. Does not smoke. Is not in debt. Is a family visitor. A peaceable man. Not addicted to long preaching. Preaches a full, free and present salvation. Is successful in the conversion of sinners to God. His conduct is good . . . He reads and studies the rules."[74] Purity was as difficult to attain and keep in isolated (but not monastic) communities as it was in the cities, and since holiness was at the root of the Methodist aim, every Travelling Preacher had to be assessed and able to preach a message which would answer the problem of man's sinful nature. This latter discipline applied, equally, to Local Preachers and Wesley's appeal to this standard is seen, in spirit, on a Primitive Methodist Plan of the Barnard Castle Branch of Hull Circuit in 1830: "Each Preacher who does not either Personally, or by Proxy, get his Appointments supplied, shall be reduced one Figure on the Plan for every neglected Appointment. No Preacher shall be allowed to officiate for another, unless he either has his name on the Plan or has a note from the Quarterly Meeting past, authorising him to speak in Public."[75]

In 1842, the Kendal Primitive Methodist Mission had 13 Societies, two of which were at Roundthwaite and Tibbygill (Teaby or Tebay). Lingering again with a statistic, we remember that the tiny hamlet of Roundthwaite had an earlier association with Benjamin Ingham. He visited it in August, 1748, from Dent (in north-west Yorkshire), and it became the opening of the door of his movement into Westmorland. Roundthwaite is only ten miles from Fox's Firbank Fell and four miles from Orton, birthplace, in 1748, of the Wesleyan Local Preacher, Stephen Brunskill; this small, lonely area thus came to be travelled by a succession of notable preachers who, within just over a century, represented a variety of ritual and doctrinal difference. The earlier fires have gone out.

Tebay and Roundthwaite were not listed in the Kendal Mission in 1849, though Grayrigg Society (half-way between Tebay and Kendal) had 4 Members. Earlier figures, reflecting Primitive Missionary interest, show that in the whole of 1841, when the Travelling Preacher's Salary was £44.4s.0d., Barnard Castle, Middleton, Mouthlock, Brough and Kendal Mission collected £26.17s.8d. for overseas work.[76] Camp Meetings, another distinctive feature of the Primitives, were continually planned in various parts of our area, including one for Brough Hill at Whitsuntide in 1840 and one for Asby Mask "if the Planmaker find it practible."[77] In June, 1867, there was to "be preaching at the low Cross in Appleby at 9 o'clock on Sunday Morning, by the two travelling preachers. And . . . A Camp Meeting on the Fair hill in the afternoon."[78] Travel expense was an obvious problem even though there were several Societies expected to help, financially. Of these, in 1840, Brough had 32 Members, Mouthlock 26, Bleatarn 3, Newbiggin 30, Kaber 5, Dufton 7, Espland Hill 8, Blackmoorgate 9 and Heights 2 (between Great Ormside and Great Asby).

Some indication of the Travelling Preacher's expenses are given in the Brough Minutes:[79]

"William Robinson, Horse and Mule, 3 days each and himself.	19s. 0d.
Tolls for the horses and cart through the various bars.	3s. 6d.
Corn . . . for the horses on the road.	2s. 2d.
Keep for three horses one night at Brough.	3s. 0d.
Mr. Saunders for horse and tolls to and from Newbiggin.	4s. 4½d.
Mr. Jersey Supper and bed at Sedburge.	1s. 6d.
Coach fare . . . Sedburge to Barnard Castle.	10s. 6d.
Expenses to Staveley, holding meeting.	5s. 0d.
Bills printing at Barnard Castle.	7s. 0d.
Postage for letters to and from.	0s. 8d.
20 Missionary boxes at 6d. each.	10s. 0d."

Had journeys been shorter, mule accommodation and bed would have been less necessary.

The Primitives built their Chapels and the Brough Circuit reported the following details to the Carlisle and Whitehaven District Meeting in 1886; pew rents were a considerable source of yearly income:[80]

Name of Chapel	Built	Cost (£)	Members	Average Attendance	Area Population	Lettable Sittings	Free Sittings
Brough	1878	807	No figure	100	600	104	126
Mouthlock	1831	150	31	140	300	94	60
Dufton	1839	Not knwn	37	90	400	70	40
North Stainmore	1868	260	31	70	300	140	60
Kaber	1859	110	37	60	200	106	70
Newbiggin	1837	100	38	110	300	100	36
Tebay	1885	630	83	140	2000	200	30
Kirkby Stephen	1865	613	50	160	4700	200	60
Spital	1865	143	24	45	120	50	50
Appleby	1874	468	58	70	2000	100	50

In these chapels and in various houses, the Brough Primitive Methodist Circuit Membership increased from 172 in 1851, to 458 in 1892 and to 355 in 1914, with a peak of 517 in June, 1893.[81] The total in 1932, as we said, was 417. Places on the Brough Primitive Methodist Circuit Plan, at the time of Union with the Wesleyan Methodists, were Brough, Mouthlock, Blackmoorgate, Dufton, North Stainmore, Kaber, Newbiggin, Tebay, Kirkby Stephen, Spital, Appleby, Brough Sowerby, Crackenthorpe and Greenholme. The number of Societies had decreased from 21 (in 1872), to 16 (in 1893) and to 13 (in 1923). At the time of Union, the Plan contained 54 Preachers (including Rev. J. E. Ruston, Pastor C. B. Simpson, two On Trial, three Exhorters and 25 Helpers). Some abbreviations on that Plan were CM (Camp Meeting), E (Evangelistic Services), T (Temperance Day) and * (Week of Prayer meetings). The text, at the top of the Plan (from Hebrews

10, verse 9), might have been heralding Methodist unity: "He taketh away the first that He may establish the second."

Some explanation of the reduced Membership by 1932 may be placed on the fact that some Primitives lost their lives in the First World War. In March, 1917, it was agreed "that a letter of condolence be sent to the bereaved mother of Gunner John Davidson, formerly a scholar in our schools at Kirkby Stephen and Appleby, who died from wounds (in) February 1917." It was also reported that Brother J. G. Collinson of the Spital Church had "died in hosptial in France from inflammation doubtless due to exposure in the trenches."[82] Emigration, too, took its toll and though the railways brought mobility, some people, finally, bought only a 'Single' ticket. The local newspaper which reported in 1868 that "the Railway wherever it goes carries advancement and civilization with it and thus Stainmore ... has been brought under the ameliorating influence of the age",[83] also said, 21 years later (with the drama that was supposed to accompany adventure), "the express train steams into Appleby to take 17 to Liverpool and thence to Canada for a new life; these include 2 Appleby young men; an Appleby young woman with 4 children (whose husband had already gone) and 4 young men from Crosby Ravensworth."[84] It is difficult to say, however, how significant Methodist emigration was, locally, in the late nineteenth and early twentieth centuries. Among the Wesleyans, 18 emigrated in 1904 (from the entire Carlisle District), 26 in 1905 and 23 in 1906.[85] At the Brough Primitive Methodist Circuit Meeting on 16.9.1859, it was agreed "that Zaccheus Young come off the Plan, He having emigrated to Australia."[86] However, even occasional emigrations obviously reduced membership and hopes in very small Societies, especially if the emigrant held office.

We must now note that, included in the Methodist Union of 1932, with the Wesleyans and Primitives (who had agreed that their particular emphases could be combined), was one other branch of Methodist outreach. This was the United Methodist Church. At the time of Union, in Great Britain, there were 729 United Methodist Ministers, 5,232 Local Preachers, 179,527 Members, 2,151 Sunday Schools, 36,474 Officers and Teachers, 223,395 Scholars and 2,900 Churches.[87] On June 9th, 1932, the Membership of the Appleby United Methodist Circuit was 106 in 7 Societies,[88] numerically the smallest part of the new Kirkby Stephen, Appleby and Tebay Circuit which was then formed. As with the Wesleyans and Primitives, we must trace the origins of this third part of the Union and see how, beyond and within our area, the 1932 Union combined different emphases into one Church, which, half a century later, had a total Membership of 487, 972, with 3,506 Ministers, 16,351 Local Preachers, and 263,311 children and young people,[89] with 643 of these Members in our area.[90] The United Methodists were born out of controversy yet, as with the Primitives, the spirit of earliest Wesleyan Methodism was not lost in ensuing schism. Lamentable but not profitless, these schisms enabled nineteenth-century Methodism to grow, still bringing religion to isolated places.

For six years after Wesley's death, the problem of the separation from the Church of England became natural Conference business and the part of the Layman in Methodism increasingly occupied the Methodist mind. Alexander Kilham, one of the Travelling Preachers who had spent some time working in Scotland, believed emphatically that the Laity ought to have a prominent share in the government of local Societies. His pamphlet entitled "The Progress of Liberty amongst the People called Methodists" and his forthright manner, caused the 1796 Conference to expel him from the Ministry and ensuing indignation led to the formation of the Methodist New Connexion in the following year. Membership of this new branch of Methodism reached 37,000 in the middle of the nineteenth century, but never more. (William Booth resigned from its Ministry in 1861 to form the Salvation Army). Ninety-five per cent of Wesleyan Methodism remained loyal to John Wesley's mainstream movement. Contemporary with the New Connexion were the Bible Christians, though these came into being less from schism than from what they would call the prompting of the Divine Spirit to preach in open-air and house. Their first Conference was at Baddash, near Launceston, in Cornwall, in 1819, and William O'Bryan, a Cornish boy once blessed by John Wesley, was their leader. They conducted pioneer work where little was being done by Anglicans or other Nonconformists and the Channel and Scilly Isles and the Isle of Wight were evangelised by them, as well as vast areas of Devon. They entered into West Cumberland in 1859, mainly immigrant miners and quarry men from Cornwall. They did not occupy the upper Eden as it had already been missioned by others.

Though the early years of nineteenth century England were decades in which democracy was much talked, three Methodist secessions during that time were little to do with political upheaval. The most audible exponent of Methodism's political attitudes was a Doctor Bunting who said that Methodism was as much opposed to democracy as to sin. Yet a democratic leaven that was beginning to work in the State was also bound to work a little in the Church,[91] especially when the Wesleyan Conference consisted entirely of Ministers. Surprisingly, it was an organ which kindled the first of these secessions after the formation of the New Connexion. Trustees at a Leeds Wesleyan Chapel wanted such an instrument for their Worship and Conference supported them over the heads of other local Methodists who did not like the musical idea. This controversy led to the formation of Protestant Methodism, in 1827, which survived until 1836. Conference power then proposed that Wesleyan Methodism should have a training college for its Ministers. With some, this was not a popular idea and was a further indication of Conference dictatorship; it led to the formation of the Wesleyan Methodist Association in 1836. This absorbed the Protestant Methodists and by 1839 it had a membership of 28,000. The European 'year of revolutions' (1848) was followed by a minor Methodist revolution in 1849. James Everett, a Wesleyan Travelling Preacher, was strongly suspected of being the inspiration of "Fly Sheets", a series of criticisms of dictatorial Wesleyan Methodist government, and was expelled — along with William Griffith and Samuel Dunn. These men, the Wesleyan Reformers, then drew support from all over the country and, together with the Wesleyan Methodist Association, formed the United Methodist Free Churches in 1857. Their combined membership was about 40,000, forming a Church which gave Ministers little authority and made sure they did not wear any distinctive clerical dress. In 1907, the United Methodist Free Churches brought 80,000 members to a union of Bible Christians and the Methodist New Connexion. That union, the United Methodist Church, entered into the work of evangelism and both at home and overseas it had considerable success. It was this United Methodist Church which also brough a numerical strength to the later union, in 1932, with Primitives and Wesleyans.

In one or two small villages in the upper Eden, one or two Wesleyan families became enchanted with the Association movement of the 1830's. John Dent, for example, became leader of a Bolton Associationist Society and used his own home for Sunday Services. The Crosby family at Kirkby Thore took Wesleyans into the Association in the same way. Joseph and Michael Craig, farming near Appleby, paid for Murton Association Chapel (built in 1841 at a cost of £100), Joseph having once been a Wesleyan Local Preacher. The first Quarterly Meeting of the Appleby Wesleyan Methodist Association was on December 21st, 1836, with a representation from 10 Places, totalling 111 Members. Appleby had 17, Bolton 17, Brampton 4, Brough 9, Dufton some, Kirkby Thore 25, Murton 10, Peaselands 6, Warcop 7 and Penrith 16. By 1852, there were 13 Places, though during 16 years of its short history, various places had begun and ceased. Netherhoff was added in 1838, Newbiggin (near Temple Sowerby), Soulby, Asby, Drybeck and Ormside were added in 1839, Maulds Meaburn in 1840, Sandford in 1845, Lowgill in 1846 and Hilton and Musgrave in 1847.[92] The Wesleyan Methodist Association Preachers Plan (Appleby Circuit, 1846) shows Appleby, Bolton, Brampton, Brough, Kirkby Thore, Murton, Netherhoff, Peaselands, Warcop, Asby, Sandford, Drybeck, Temple Sowerby, Maulds Meaburn, Musgrave and Hilton as "Places". It advertises Collections, Sacraments, Ticket distribution, Lovefeasts and the Quarterly Meeting, with special reference to a Camp Meeting at which Mr. Bailiff of Kirkby Thore and Mr. Nicholson and Mr. Williamson of Appleby are "to attend". Clearly the formation of this Circuit, with fifteen accredited preachers and five On Trial, in 1846, must have been a drain on Wesleyan resources. We note, in passing, the practice of the Primitive Methodist Camp Meeting. That the Circuit was formed at all showed a strong, if temporary, phase of anti-Wesleyanism. That it took almost another century before it could be re-absorbed into a wider Methodism was something of a local, even national tragedy. The building programme and other indications of local commitment in 9 Societies is set out in the following table:[93]

Chapel	Year Built	Cost (£)	Seats	Afternoon Attendance	Evening Attendance	Sittings Let
Appleby	1870	800	200	142 (morning)	81	66
Colby Maulds	1874	200	72	25	25	None
Meaburn	1878	245	100	54	39	24
Murton	1841	100	82	34	18	34
Warcop	1844	120	80	42	30	28
Sandford	1848	90	70	41	None	6
Bolton	1818	-	130	30	60	None
Kirkby Thore	1851	150	120	88	35	None
Asby	1859	140	120	40	None	None

In the *Register of the names of the Members of the Wesleyan Methodist Association in the Appleby Circuit, commencing in 1840 December 21st,* there are various illuminating remarks concerning the Members of the places where there were Societies; some of them add further insights on emigration while others help to paint a picture of this Eden valley movement which was strongest around the County Town of Appleby:

"1844. Full Members returned to Assembly, 150.
1850. William Slee Joined Ranters. (i.e. Primitives).
Thomas Dobinson Gone to America some time ago.
1852. 137 Full Members.
1853. Susan Hoskin Left Connexion.
Bridget Dent Gone to Heaven. 130 Full Members.
1854. 152 Full Members. 2 Deaths, 7 Backsliders and 10 Removals.
1860. William, Elizabeth and Joseph Steele at Shepherd's Cottage, near Murton emigrated to Australia.
1861. John Horn dropt. (sic).
William Sewell Backslidden through drink."

In 1867 there was a Revival at Appleby, with 171 Members in the Circuit; there was one Itinerant Preacher, 20 Local Preachers, 11 Leaders, 7 Chapels, 3 Preaching Rooms, 6 Sunday Schools, 281 Scholars and 63 Teachers. In further United Methodist Free Church Registers, we note:

"1870. William Atkinson Removed to America.
1872. Elizabeth Davyes Gone to America.
1893. Jane Fairer Joined Wesleyans.
Alfred Davidson Removed to America.
1897. Martha Best Gone to America.
1909. W. and I. Slinger and H. and A. Stephenson to Canada.
1918. John Lambert Killed in Action."

Emigrants do not add up to any large number but we wonder what happens to the religion of a small Society when someone leaves it, forever. Does the leader of that Society lose some of his authority because he may think that the emigrant's religious need drove him away? Even if (and more likely) reason for emigration was economic, did the Methodists left behind feel a loss of identity? Do small isolated groups, therefore, seek for larger unions as they see their numbers dwindle or do they become more eager to evangelize to make up the losses? Was there a link between loss through emigration and interest in missionary activity overseas, attempting to win back whatever had been lost?

A *Baptismal Register for Appleby Tabernacle United Methodist Free Church* (1850-1932) shows the occupations of parents in the Circuit to be so varied as to make one wonder if their religious affiliation was as strong as the variety was widespread. Butter dealer, waller, miller, mason, coachman, clothier, miner, day-school teacher, Royal Mail Driver, wheelwright, nailer, groom, chemist, carter, butcher, builder, tailor, dressmaker, plate layer and draper (between 1866 and 1880) all suggest a remarkable connection between this branch of Methodism and society as a whole. In the same Register, which contains Marriage entries from 1850 to 1877, partners come from as far away as Berwick-on-Tweed, Sunderland and Darlington. Visitors, for Baptims, come from Manchester (1886 and 1887), Carlisle (1890), Aberdeenshire (1893), Fort William (1905), Morecambe (1909), Castleford (1916) and Doncaster (1929). It would seem that Infant Baptism was probably offered to any who requested it, and parents, who may not have been committed Christians, thus made a nominal entrance into an isolated holy community. On the other hand, Baptism may have been sought for children of a parent, or parents, who once belonged to local Methodism but had been then forced by circumstances to go and live far from the upper Eden valley.

The Quarterly Meeting Minutes of the Wesleyan Methodist Association shed light on their ways and reflected that whatever their attitudes to the Wesleyan Methodist Conference, their aims were those of John Wesley. On December 27th, 1848, they agreed, at Appleby, that "a series of revival Services be held in several of our Chapels and other places to commence on New Year's Eve." They also wanted to belong to a wider Association. "We think it advisable to adopt District Meetings and we hope the Annual Assembly will take it into consideration."[94] But their own Circuit affairs were naturally paramount: "this meeting approves of the Methodistic mode of giving out the Hymns and it would kindly recommend the various Societies to adopt that method. With special reference to Appleby, they be requested to adopt singing as a substitute for their usual manner of chanting."[95] The Circuit resolved "to remit no more monies to the Connexion Funds, until our own demand be attended to. And that the surplus be remitted."[96] There was no reference to the new union, in 1857, forming the United Methodist Free Church, but earlier minutes suggested happy approval of the proposition. Though smaller in number than Wesleyans or Primitives, their vision still extended beyond the local area, when, in 1862, the Quarterly Meeting resolved "that collections be made toward the relief of the Members of our own churches in the manufacturing districts suffering on account of the Cotton famine in all our chapels and meeting houses in the Circuit."[97] By 1926, the United Methodist Church had, in spite of the union of 1907, its own financial difficulties. The Quarterly Meeting "resolved that a special quarterly meeting be held when the question of finance be fully discussed. Our isolated situation was stressed, and the steward suggested that we should have a debt of £180 by June next."[98] In 1930, finance still troubled the United Methodist Circuit and it was decided after much discussion, "to Carry on and do the best possible until organic union of the 3 Churches is fully accomplished."[99] Even so, there were other advantages to a united Church which Reverend C. E. Ward, a Wesleyan Minister, stressed when he was invited to the United Methodist Church Quarterly Meeting at Colby: "Though of a Different outlook Temprement (sic) the 3 Societies Could be so blended into one that the spirit of the Master would be better revealed to the world."[100] At the last United Methodist Quarterly Meeting, the visionary Minute read that they hoped it would "be the commencement of a larger Methodism."[101]

The last phase of Methodist occupation of the upper Eden, beginning in 1932, was thus to have a more united strategy, even though it hardly became "a larger Methodism": the combined Circuit Membership, in 1932, of 1,250 was, by 1982, reduced to 643. We recall that 106 United Methodists (in 7 Societies) had united with 417 Primitive Methodists (in 14 Societies) and with 727 Wesleyan Methodists (in 26 Societies). There were (in October, 1982) a total of thirty four Societies. The membership had been reduced by 50% and the Societies, all with Chapels, were reduced by 28%, the area covered being as wide as ever. In 1982, Anglican Places of Worship in the same area were 17, that is half the number of Chapels. There were three Methodist Ministers in the Kirkby Stephen, Appleby and Tebay Circuit, but seven Anglican clergymen covering approximately the same area. The two largest Methodist Societies were Appleby (with 100 Members) and Kirkby Stephen (with 80); 15 of the Societies had memberships of less than 10. The remaining 17 Societies had an average membership of 22. Spital, furthest east, bleak and lonely, had 7 Members, still keeping its association with the "West Country", a title it ascribed to the Circuit which sent its Preachers onto this Pennine summit. All its Members, however, lived *east* of Spital — mostly in Barnard Castle — and in August, 1984, it ceased to be used as a building for Methodist Worship.

Official Methodist business at local Society level was often infrequent and sparsely minuted. Sometimes, therefore, Trustees' Minutes began before Methodist Union and continued long afterwards. A Gaisgill Wesleyan Trust Minute Book contains business as early as 1900 and as late as 1953.[102] Similarly, Brough Primitive Methodist Circuit Third Baptismal Register began as the Primitive Register for Appleby, Dufton, Crackenthorpe, Grassgill and Brough district and dates from 1900 to 1960.[103] Individual Chapel Trust Minutes say less about the growth of

Methodism in the upper Eden than do Baptismal Registers and, as with the United Methodists, it is noticeable that parents came from several corners of society for their child's Baptism into particular Methodist Congregations. After 1932, there is a poultry farmer and a meal traveller (1936), confectioner (1937), quarry worker, council roadman, electric worker (1939), journalist, school teacher, night watchman, H.M. Forces, forestry worker, navy (1942), electrical engineer (1944), bank clerk, taxi proprietor (1946), taxi-driver (1948), fish salesman, maintenance engineer (1949), architect (1950), van driver, regular army (1956) and lorry driver (1957). These are among the greater number of farmers but lead us to wonder whether, at the very point of initiation, Methodist practice was too all-embracing if and when it permitted non-Methodist parents to take part in the Baptismal rite. The Registers do not, of course, confirm whether particular parents were committed Methodists or not, any more than the Registers of St. Lawrence's Church, Appleby, can confirm that the partents of five Romany babies, "christened" during the Horse Fair in June, 1972, were committed Members of the Church of England.[104]

Although by 1952 the local weekly newspaper's continued interest in Methodism for nearly 100 years seemed to be waning (when sport, politics, agriculture and the Women's Institute were becoming more newsworthy), the journalism of 20 years earlier drew considerable attention to Methodist Union. On September 17th, 1932, it said that thousands of Methodists would be gathering in their Churches on Tuesday (September 20th) to listen to the historic broadcast of the inauguration of Church Union from the Royal Albert Hall, which would be attended by the Duke and Duchess of York. Indeed, 10,000 acclaimed the Union and the King sent a message noticing this "Step towards unity of all Christian people." On the platform were the Bishop of London and three ex-Presidents, the Duke and Duchess of York, the Mayor of Westminster, Sir Robert Perks (the new Conference Vice President) and Dr. Scott Lidgett (the new President).[105] One turns into October's *Herald* to find stimulating 'Union' correspondence but the letters are headed "Penrith Butchers and their Prices", "Catching Rabbits by Human Methods" and "Tombstones and Beauty",[106] their common theme being death rather than comment on an event of some national importance.

The *Herald* also reported local Methodism's continued interest in Missionary work. The District Synod at Penrith heard how the Kirkby Stephen, Appleby and Tebay Circuit had shown the largest increase in Missionary giving,[107] while at Dufton Methodist Chapel the meaningfulness of local interest was reflected in the Address of Miss Sowbhagium Kondiah, Principal of the Wesley Girls' High School at Secunderabad, in South India,[108] who visited the Society in person. An an annual Guild Rally at the Sands Methodist Chapel, Appleby, in 1962, the speaker was a Mr. F. Webb who was on furlough from Peru; Kirkby Stephen, Crosby, Ravensworth, Tebay and Kirkby Thore were all represented.[109]

A week-by-week glance at the *Herald* through the whole of 1981, reminds the reader of a Methodism which is still a prominent feature of Eden society and the following are four significant extracts and references:

1. "Mr. Ebenezer Robert Harris, who died recently, aged 89 years, was well known in the area, having preached in many local chapels in the last 60 years. He was the last of the family of Stephen Brunskill Harris, who was grandson of Stephen Brunskill, of Orton, who became a Christian through the preaching of John Wesley." (p. 5, col. 4, 18.4.1981).

2. In a letter regarding Church Unity from the Reverend E. D. Hodgkiss, one of the three Circuit Ministers, she stated: "We believe that God — who loves and creates variety — raised the various denominations up to fulfil His specific purpose. We are not persuaded that those purposes are now ended." (p, 7, col. 2, 20.6.1981).

3. In contrast with first Wesleyan, Primitive and United Methodist Harvest Festivals (which were held to increase local Circuit funds), new signs of Missionary interest were reported. Bolton Methodists sent £112 from their Harvest Festival to help needy people in the Third World (p. 2, col. 5, 26.9.1981), as did Winton, a week later, by contributing £176 to the same fund (p. 2, col. 4, 3.10.1981).

4. On the death of Mr. L. S. Chapman, whose loyalty to the Circuit had been outstanding, he was described as "a staunch Methodist". He had combined his work as a Circuit Steward with that of a Headmaster in Appleby for 34 years and with that of Mayor, Alderman and Magistrate. (p. 12, cols. 1-3, 12.2.1981).

The *Herald* also gives us some idea of the relationship between Methodists and Anglicans over the years, two branches of the Christian Church which now exist, side by side, in organic isolation. John Wesley would not have wanted this, but even in his lifetime it became apparent that Methodists were being separated from the Church of England. Some Anglicans encouraged persecution of Methodists in Wesley's lifetime and Conferences after 1791 could do nothing to prevent a final break. Attitudes varied from Parish to Parish, though encouraging news came from Penrith in 1867: "A United Prayer Meeting was held in the Working Men's Reading Room. The Rev. G. C. Hodgson, Vicar of Barton, opened the meeting with suitable portions of Scripture. Then the Rev. T. T. Dilks, Wesleyan, and the Rev. W. Brewis, Independent, and the Rev. J. Dodd, Primitive, Mr. Bell, and Mr. James Irving engaged in prayer. The large number who attended the meeting must have afforded great encouragement to these Ministers and gentlemen who have taken an effective part in its establishment."[110] A fanciful notion was, however, destroyed in the same town in the following year, when, in a lecture entitled "The people called Methodists" given by a Reverend H. Newbson from Appleby (as the local newspaper reported), "he referred to the opinion of some churchmen who seemed to think that Methodists could be brought into communion with the Church by making their places of Worship chapels of ease. The Reverend lecturer concluded by expressing an opinion that there was not the remotest possibility of the Wesleyan Methodists being absorbed in the Church of England."[111] Such a conviction appears to have been widespread, for we find that Dr. Rigg, an ex-President of the Wesleyan Conference, lamented that Church of

England Clergymen had left the platforms of meetings and committees connected with the Bible Society. They were beginning to look at Nonconformists as people to be avoided; they were hoping to see an end of Churches like the Methodist Church whom they regarded as schismatics.[112] Yet, at Tebay, ten years later, we find a different situation. At the annual Railway Servants Camp Meeting, Services began with public prayer in the Primitive Methodist Schoolroom on a Saturday evening, continued on Sunday morning at 7 a.m., after which there was Holy Communion in the Parish Church at 8 a.m. Then a procession was formed at Old Tebay and another at the Railway Station at 9 a.m., both uniting near the Church at 10.15 a.m. after which they dispersed, some going to the Church and others to the Chapel where separate services were held. Collections were made in Church, Chapel and Market Hall in aid of the Camp Meeting Fund, the surplus to be divided amongst the widows of deceased railway servants.[113] James Graham, however, of Kirkby Stephen, wrote to the editor of the *Mid-Cumberland and North Westmorland Herald* in 1899 to say that "Where the clergy is not intolerant there is little fault to find but in very many cases our children are treated with the greatest injustice. They are taught that ours is not a Church, that our Ministers are only laymen, that our Sacraments are an imposture, that Dissent is sin and in the most subtle form they are influenced to look down upon Nonconformity."[114] As ever, attitudes varied unexpectedly. At Askham, near Penrith, the Anglican and Wesleyan Sunday Schools decided to meet together because of a shortage of Wesleyan Sunday School teachers. Both Churches also agreed unanimously to the revolutionary idea of monthly united Worship.[115] The First World War had just come to an end and it was sensible for the Reverend H. O. Briggs, Superintendent of the Penrith Wesleyan Circuit to say in a Sermon: "To deal with all the world's problems, the world's social relationships, the great Colour question, and the world's evangelization, the Church needed unity of counsel and unity of command."[116] The Reverend J. E. Rattenbury, a Methodist speaking at Alston, asked the pertinent question: "If the Church, which professed friendship, could not unite how could the world unite?"[117] By 1942, another war had superseded such a vision and news from Ravenstonedale was as significant as Askham's ventures of earlier days: the Anglicans, Congregationalists and Methodists agreed to hold monthly weeknight Services.[118]

The Brough Primitive Methodist Circuit Minute Book, however, confirms that there were sometimes disturbing situations: "It having come to our knowledge that the Reverend A. Warren (Bongdate, Appleby), in his capacity as clergyman of the parish, has been endeavouring to get some of our Sunday School scholars to be confirmed or to attend Church Sunday School, we hereby authorise our Minister to write him on behalf of this official meeting, pointing out to him that this kind of thing is most objectionable to us, and we ask him kindly to refrain from doing so in the future. [119] Twelve years later, such problems arose again: "Having heard on reliable authority, it is the practice of certain clergymen to get children attending our Sunday Schools to be confirmed and become adherents of the Established Church, and that veiled attacks are sometimes made upon our Church in the course of such proselytising, we enter our protest against this practice, and consider it desirable, in the interests of our schools, that the fullest publicity be given to cases coming under our notice in future."[120] But a better note was sounded in United Methodist Minutes at the Appleby Circuit Local Preachers' Meeting and Quarterly Meeting on June 21st, 1906: "A letter was read from W. J. E. Thompson of Maulds Meaburn regarding the vicar of Crosby Ravensworth's willingness to conduct a Service in the Maulds Meaburn Church and that his name appear on the Plan as a Helper. Resolved that the arrangement between the Vicar of Crosby Ravensworth and W. J. E. Thompson be respected as an exchange of Preachers."[121] Friendly or estranged, the two branches of the Christian Church existed side by side, but, for Methodism, conversions were to become essential and, for that reason alone, the upper Eden valley was to come out of the darkness of the Druid wood into the light of new, transforming beliefs: shared openly and shared together.

---

[1] A. W. Harrison, B. A. Barber, G. G. Hornby and E. T. Davies *The Methodist Church. Its Origin, Divisions and Renunion* (London, 1932), p. 12.

[2] *Ibid.*, p. 13.

[3] John Wesley, *The Journal*, V, 283-284.

[4] *Ibid.*, V, 192.

[5] They had an inner compulsion to do this.

[6] Methodist Publishin House (London, 1981).

[7] *The Constitutional Practice and Discipline of the Methodist Church*, pp. 523-525.

[8] John Wesley, *The Journal*, III, 143-144.

[9] *Ibid.*, III, 143-144, note 2.

[10] *Ibid.*, III, 196, note 3.

[11] Dr. Coke and Mr. Moore, *The Life of the Reverend John Wesley*, A.M. (London, 1792), pp. 58-59.

[12] Cyril J. Davey, *The Methodist Story*, (London, 1955), p. 23.

[13] Minutes of Whitehaven *Wesleyan District* Meeting, 29.5.1804.

[14] *Ibid.*, 17.7.1805.

[15] *The Methodist Church*, p. 43.

[16] By the Conference Plan of Pacification in 1795.

[17] John Bond, *Golden Candlesticks, or sketches of the rise of some early Methodist Churches* (London, 1873), p. 85.

[18] *History of Methodism in Barnard Castle*, p. 27.

[19] *Ibid.*, p. 30.

[20] *Ibid.*, p. 56.

[21] *Ibid.*, pp. 58-59.

[22] *The Life of Stephen Brunskill of Orton*, p. 6. Richard Brunskill, married, of Winton, had been received into membership of the Birks Inghamite Society, at a Lovefeast, on October 28th, *1759* (according to the Minutes of the *Inghamites*, 1755-1760).

[23] *History of Methodism in Barnard Castle*, pp. 78-79.

[24] Local pronunciation of 'Melmerby'.

[25] *History of Methodism in Barnard Castle*, pp. 87-88: to the north and east of our area.

[26] *Ibid.*, pp. 111-112.

[27] John Wesley, *The Journal*, V, 472.

[28] *History of Methodism in Barnard Castle*, p. 118.

[29] *Ibid.*, p. 178.

[30] *Ibid.*, p. 189 (see p. 9).

[31] and [32] Farmhouses in the Great Asby area.

[33] *History of Methodism in Barnard Castle*, p. 192.

[34] *Ibid.*, p. 193.

[35] Minutes of the *Wesleyan District Meeting*, 1.7.1812; the District is then known as the CARLISLE District.

[36] *Ibid.*, 8.7.1818.

[37] *Ibid.*, 31.5.1820.

[38] *Ibid.*, 30.5.1821.
[39] *Ibid.*, 13.5.1823.
[40] *Ibid.*, 26/27.5.1824.
[41] *Ibid.*, 24/25.5.1825.
[42] That is, the Appleby Wesleyan Circuit Quarterly Meeting.
[43] Minutes of *Carlisle Wesleyan District Meeting*, 28/29.5.1828.
[44] *Ibid.*, 30.5.1832.
[45] J. Thompson and E. Thompson, in the list of Preachers, are also in the list of subscribers at Long Marton in 1841; see p. 30. of this thesis.
[46] John Wesley, *The Journal*, III, 307.
[47] John Wesley, *The Letters of the Rev. John Wesley, A.M.* (London, 1931), VI, 224.
[48] Minutes of the *Carlisle Wesleyan District Meeting*, 19.5.1840.
[49] *Ibid.*, May 1842.
[50] *Ibid.*, May 1844.
[51] John Wesley, *The Letters*, VI, 215.
[52] Minutes of the *Carlisle Wesleyan District Meeting*, 1875 (Question 19).
[53] When it united with other branches of the Methodist movement.
[54] *The Methodist Church*, p. 229.
[55] Minutes of the *Brough Primitive Methodist Circuit Quarterly Meeting*, 1.12.1932.
[56] *Circuit Schedule Book of the Kirkby Stephen and Appleby Wesleyan Circuit* (June, 1932).
[57] *The Methodist Story*, p. 106.
[58] Joseph Ritson, *The Romance of Primitive Methodism* (London, 1909), p. 12.
[59] *Ibid.*, pp. 52-53.
[60] *Rules and Regulations for the Societies of the Primitive Methodist Connexion* (M. R. Publishing, Leigh-on-Sea, 1975) Methodist Reprints, No. 2, p. 1.
[61] W. M. Patterson, *Northern Primitive Methodism* (London, 1909), pp. 103-104.
[62] *Ibid.*, p. 104.
[63] *Ibid.*, p. 113.
[64] *Ibid.*, p. 116.
[65] *The Primitive Methodist Magazine* (London, 1842), p. 32.
[66] *Ibid.*, 1855, p. 327.
[67] *Ibid.*, 1861, p. 381.
[68] *Ibid.*, 1855, p. 328.
[69] *Ibid.*, 1848, p. 571.
[70] H. B. Kendall, "Primitive Methodist Church" in W. J. Townsend, H. B. Workman and G. Eayrs, ed., *A New History of Methodism* (London, 1909) I, 580.
[71] *Statistics from The Account Book of the Reverend William Harland*, Primitive Methodist Travelling Preacher (1831-1842).
[72] Minutes of the *Barnard Castle Primitive Methodist Circuit Quarterly Meeting* (Report to District), 1841.
[73] *Ibid.*, 1844.
[74] *Ibid.*, 1841.
[75] Joseph Hawkins, *O'er Hill and Dale and by the Solway Shore* (Watton, Norfolk, 1907), p. 72.
[76] Quarter Day Account and Minute Book of *Brough Primitive Methodist Branch of the Hull Circuit* (12.12.1841).
[77] Minutes of the *Brough Primitive Methodist Circuit Quarterly Meeting*, 3.3.1840.
[78] *Ibid.*, 15.6.1867, Resolution 24.
[79] *Ibid.*, 8.12.1840.
[80] *Ibid.*, 1886.
[81] These figures are from the *Brough Primitive Methodist Quarter-day Account Books* for the years mentioned.
[82] Minutes of the *Brough Primitive Methodist Circuit Quarterly Meeting*, 1.3.1917.
[83] *Cumberland and Westmorland Advertiser*, 1.12.1868.
[84] *Ibid.*, 25.6.1889.
[85] Minutes of the *Carlisle Wesleyan District Meeting*, 1906.
[86] Minutes of the *Brough Primitive Methodist Circuit Quarterly Meeting*, 1859.
[87] *The Methodist Church*, p. 229.
[88] Minutes of the *Appleby United Methodist Circuit Quarterly Meeting*, 9.6.1932.
[89] *Annual Report of the Free Church Federal Council* (London, 1982), p. 28.
[90] *Plan and Directory* of the Kirkby Stephen, Appleby and Tebay Circuit: October-December, 1982.
[91] *The Methodist Church*, p. 146.
[92] Minutes of the *Appleby Wesleyan Methodist Association Circuit Quarterly Meetings*.
[93] *Special Schedule for 1881: United Methodist Free Church Societies*. By 1929 there were only seven of these Societies: Appleby, Colby, Maulds Meaburn, Sandford, Bolton, Kirkby Thore and Great Asby.
[94] Minutes of the *Wesleyan Methodist Association Circuit Quarterly Meeting*, 26.7.1851.
[95] *Ibid.*, 29.9.1852.
[96] *Ibid.*, 29.9.1852.
[97] *Ibid.*, 24.9.1862.
[98] *Ibid.*, 3.6.1926.
[99] *Ibid.*, 27.2.1930.
[100] *Ibid.*, 11.12.1930.
[101] *Ibid.*, 24.8.1933.
[102] Minutes of the *Gaisgill Wesleyan Trustees Meetings*.

[103] *Baptismal RegistersL* Brough Primitive Methodist Circuit, 1900-1960 (No. 3).
[104] *Cumberland and Westmorland Herald*, 17.6.1972.
[105] *Ibid.*, 17/24.9.1932.
[106] *Ibid.*, 15.10.1932.
[107] *Ibid.*, 16.5.1942.
[108] *Ibid.*, 7.6.1952.
[109] *Ibid.*, 19.5.1962.
[110] *Cumberland and Westmorland Advertiser*, 15.1.1867.
[111] *Ibid.*, 25.2.1868.
[112] *Ibid.*, 11.11.1879; in an address at Truro
[113] *Ibid.*, 23.7.1889.
[114] *Mid-Cumberland and North Westmorland Herald*, 18.2.1899.
[115] *Ibid.*, 8.3.1919.
[116] *Ibid.*, 22.3.1919.
[117] *Ibid.*, 21.6.1919.
[118] *Cumberland and Westmorland Herald*, 24.10.1942.
[119] Minutes of the *Brough Primitive Methodist Circuit Preachers' Meeting*, 4.3.1897.
[120] *Ibid.*, 4.3.1909.
[121] Minutes of the *Appleby United Methodist Circuit Quarterly Meeting*, 21.6.1906.

CHAPTER III

Never The Same Again

There is no reason to doubt that what Methodists thought and believed elsewhere, they also believed in the upper Eden valley. This new phenomenon of living religion, born out of individual conversions, was the expression of community beliefs, and though Wesley had advised on essential private acts of devotion, Methodism was clearly about meeting with fellow-believers. "Nature and the devil will always oppose private prayer" he wrote,[1] and an individual convert has to ensure that "in retirement or company, in leisure, business, or conversation, his heart is ever with the Lord."[2] But, writing to Frances Godfrey, on August 2nd, 1789, he also said "I hope you find satisfaction ... in some of your Christian companions. It is a blessed thing to have fellow travellers to the New Jerusalem. If you cannot find any, you must make them; for none can travel that road alone. Then labour to help each other so that you may be altogether Christians."[3] In houses, in chapels and in the open-air Methodists therefore met together. It was the only way in which the essential community impression could be made and the only atmosphere in which new Methodists could grow towards holiness. "Let us join" was a repeated theme in Charles Wesley's hymns, urging Methodists to "travel on together."[4] When, in 1837, Hodgson Casson (1788-1851), a Wesleyan Travelling Preacher from Workington, said "Methodism wants no mending; it only wants keeping and practising,"[5] he meant that it should be kept and practised together, otherwise it was a solitary religion and of such there was nothing in Holy Scripture.[6] We shall now see, therefore, ways in which Eden Methodists came together, making particular reference to preaching, fellowship, teaching, singing, missionary and Guild meetings, and the Band of Hope. In all, the over-riding purposes were evangelism and holiness. This other Eden could never be the same again after its discovery by these Methodists.

In reply to Dr. Gibson, Bishop of London, in 1747, Wesley declared the supreme importance of preaching. "Here are in and near Moorfields ten thousand poor souls, for whom Christ died, rushing headlong into hell. Is Dr. Bulkeley, the parochial minister, both willing and able to stop them? If so, let it be done, and I have no place in these parts: I go and call other sinners to repentance. But if, after all he has done and all he can do, they are still in the broad way to destruction, let me see if God will put a word even in my mouth."[7] "Wherever I see one or a thousand men running into hell, be it in England, Ireland or France, yes, in Europe, Asia, Africa, or America, I will stop them if I can ... Were I to do otherwise, were I to let any soul drop into the pit whom I might have saved from everlasting burnings, I am not satisfied God would accept my plea, 'Lord, he was not of my parish'."[8] To Charles Perronet, he wrote: "If we could once bring all our preachers, itinerant and local, uniformly and steadily to insist on those two points, 'Christ dying for us' and 'Christ reigning in us', we should shake the trembling gates of hell."[9] Fear of hell and Satan were realities to both the Wesleys, and Charles gave the only answer:

"Jesus! the name that charms our fears."[10]

The manipulative power of Satan had a dangerous charm of its own, which, like the sorcery of African traditional religion, might devour human souls.[11] Charles Wesley's fervent prayer thus became:

> "Thy love, let it my heart o'erpower
> And all my simple soul devour"[12]

In the Poetical Works of the Wesleys, we read:

> "Satan must tremble and give place
> Before the Spirit's might,
> The strength of efficacious grace
> Puts all his hosts to flight;
> His kingdom falls, his charms and spells
> And works are all o'erthrown,
> When Jesus in the faithful dwells
> And rules their hearts alone."[13]

The besom (or barsom?) would finally destroy Satan's most treasured possession, for, as the Methodist poets also wrote:

> "Satan his kingdom's fall shall see,
> Its final period sin shall feel,
> Destruction shall the besom be,
> And sweep its last remains to hell."[14]

Thus it was that this compulsion to preach spread to the upper Eden, through Wesley's Travelling Preachers and their converts. When Hodgson Casson, who had been a Travelling preacher in the Brough Wesleyan Circuit between 1819 and 1821, went to Gateshead in 1827, it seemed that there, in the town, Satan would be more active. "Leaving the inhabitants of the dales in their scattered dwellings, where they were comparatively shut out from much of that contaminating influence, which, like a moral pestilence, stalks along in places more densely populated, poisoning the life-blood of society, he had now, in the order of Providence, to plant his battering-rams in a place 'where Satan's seat' was."[15] But Wesleyan Conferences knew that preaching was as necessary in rural areas as in cities and indication of this is found in the *Kirkby Stephen and Appleby Wesleyan Circuit Local Preachers' Minutes (1908-1924)* into which the printed rules and regulations of various Conferences, relating to Local Preachers, have been bound. The 1796 Conference had said (p. 5 of these Rules and

Regulations) that all Local Preachers must meet in Class. In the spirit of the 1820 Conference (p. 8), we read that "in order to revive and increase small and decaying congregations, especially in villages", we should "have recourse to the practice of preaching out of doors; going to those who need us most; and seeking, by all means, to gather into the House of God them that are lost." The 1869 Conference (p. 5) had directed that "no Preacher be permitted to preach in any Circuit than his own without consent of the Superintendent of that Circuit" and (on p. 6) Conference Minutes of 1876 and 1895, in an attempt to train Local Preachers, had said that "No Candidate shall be fully admitted as a Local Preacher until he has read the Fifty-three Standard Sermons of Mr. Wesley, and his Notes on the New Testament, and until he has passed a satisfactory examination in the definitions and Scripture proofs of the leading doctrines of Christianity as there explained."

Stephen Brunskill of Orton shows how he became a preacher, the connection between preaching and forming Societies then being particularly important since, as John Wesley had said, "no regular societies, no discipline, no order or connexion; and the consequence is that nine in ten of the once-awakened are now faster asleep than ever."[16]

"On Christmas Day (1774)", writes Brunskill in his autobiography, "after receiving the Sacrament of the Lord's Supper, I met the Class in the evening. After I had done, I gave a word of exhortation in which I found considerable freedom. After speaking a few times in this way my father invited his neighbours and I began to exhort more publicly. The first time I took a text was in my own house. The People were deeply affected, many tears being shed. My beginning to preach was soon made known among the little societies at a distance and I was invited to visit them and preach to them the word of life. The Word of God was precious in those days and preachers very scarce. So little did the people know about a Sermon that if a preacher could only get on and be lively, he was sure to be well received. This was much in my favour and my feeble efforts were owned of God. Several were awakened to a sense of their danger and a few I believe were converted to God. They were formed into little Societies and soon afterwards visited by the Travelling Preachers."[17]

This was the way local preaching began and Brunskill speaks of the way it spread:

"We rented a room in Orton as a place of religious Worship and several persons were brought to God. Among the rest was Mr. Barnes well-known among the Methodists in Manchester. Also his father, mother and three brothers. In Ravenstonedale also the work of God prospered and sinners were saved. It was here that Mr. Thomas Shaw was brough to a saving knowledge of the Truth who afterwards became a Travelling Preacher. During the four years he laboured in that capacity he was the honoured instrument of bringing many souls to God."[18]

He also refers to holiness, Wesley's second preaching theme — "Christ reigning in us":

"Some of the Preachers strongly enforced the doctrine of Christian Perfection but I did not understand nor could I comprehend it, but felt my mind prejudiced against it until I read the life of Martha Thompson, when my prejudice was removed and I saw its amiableness and that it was my privilege to enjoy it. I therefore began to seek it with all my heart and it was not long till the Lord heard and answered prayer by bringing my soul under the purifying influence of divine grace and enabling me to rejoice in the perfect love of God. But I did not retain this great blessing long for being in a great measure ignorant of Satan's devices he soon robbed me of it. Yet I never again felt that opposition to the will of God which I had sometimes formerly done but on the contrary a general submission thereto although I had in a measure lost my evidence of sanctification."[19]

Stephen Brunskill,[20] untypical of Eden valley Local Preachers in that he had opportunity to write an informative autobiography, was one faithful messenger among the many who, for two centuries, continued to preach where Travelling Preachers could not often come. "Methodist work in the villages," it was said (a century after Brunskill) "would be impossible but for the immense numbers of local preachers who for Christ's sake voluntarily and at their own cost serve the pulpits of the Connexion. A large proportion of them come from the country, and are strong men who can drive a straight furrow and describe the ways of God, but who have never had the chance of acquiring much secular knowledge."[21] This was why the Wesleyan Conference made its rules for Local Preachers and why, too, the Primitives expected their preachers to read and study other books apart from, but related to, the Holy Scriptures. "No person's name shall appear on the Plan until he has been examined . . . The examination shall be based on the following books: (1) Holy Scriptures; (2) Gregory's Theological Student; (3) Gill's Grammar; (4) Consolidated Minutes; (5) Kendall's History of the Connexion . . . ."[22] The present Methodist Conference continues this careful tradition of ensuring that preachers who occupy its pulpits — anywhere in the Connexion — have reached a standard of Biblical and theological understanding and have an awareness of what is best in pulpit manner and conduct of Worship. Once a preacher becomes "fully accredited", he must attend all the quarterly Circuit Preachers' meetings. (Preachers "On Trial" must only be present in these meetings when the business does not relate to them in particular). Preachers must accept the disciplines of the Conference and continue to learn how to share in the proclamation of the Gospel. They must still be Members of the Methodist Church and walk worthily of their calling. They are still under the direction of their Superintendent Minister for their preaching appointments. Their message is still to be that of John Wesley: new life for all.

Once a "man in the pew" listens to a compelling preacher and makes a positive response, he can never be the same again. He has associated with a group of people who have convictions about life and death. These are different from those of his non-committed neighbour, if, that is, his neighbour has any views at all. If he belongs to a small such group, in a rural hamlet or village, he is therefore particularly isolated, not from his fellow-Methodist, but from his society who will watch critically for strong evidence of his change of heart. Joseph Grieves, "profane, drunkard and poacher" was just such a man. He attended a prayer-meeting in Teesdale (a valley running parallel with the upper Eden, some 13 miles to the North-East) in 1823 and this is what happened: "In the course of the prayer-meeting the Holy Ghost went through my heart like a burning flame. I... attempted to stop the praying. The preacher, John Hewson, came out of the pulpit and cried 'Believe! Believe!' I shouted 'I do believe' and from that hour I never doubted my acceptance with God."[23] Grieves, with three fellow-converts, at once began preaching and "their old companions in sin went to hear these unlettered men pray and talk about religion and the rough Teesdale lead miners were the means of promoting a gracious work in the place."[24] A true 'Chapel man' was almost without blemish and his new life-style was a Sermon in itself: one sermon led to another.

Christopher Kearton who died at Brough, in 1866, when he was 74, was one such "chapel man". For more than 40 years of his early life he was a swearing man, a Sabbath profaner and kept "worldly-minded" company. At the age of 42 he was persuaded to go to Mouthlock Primitive Methodist Chapel. He there "felt and owned his guilt and shortly afterwards while wrestling alone with God in earnest, believing prayer, deliverance came. He obtained peace with God... In those days and in this neighbourhood the labourers in the Gospel field were few in number. Accordingly, brother Kearton was soon called by the Church to fill the important office of Local Preacher which he did for upwards of 30 years with credit to himself and profit to his hearers." Not that every Local Preacher had his pre-conversion sins listed. John Dickinson, for example, who died in 1905, was described as a prosperous business man who always attended his weeknight prayer meeting and Preaching Service. "For over 40 years he tramped with unwearying zeal the dales and the moors of the Brough Circuit (one of the widest in the Connexion touching on three counties) with the message of the Cross and often delivered that message to a very small Congregation after travelling many miles... He was one of the makers of rural Primitive Methodism in the County of Westmorland and no one had an intenser regard for the small village Society than he ... ."[26] George Jackson, a Primitive Methodist from Tebay (1806-1879), experienced "the birth from above" but he, too, had been drinker and dancer, living where "foolish games such as wrestling, racing, and playing at football on the Sabbath-day" used to take place. Converted in 1832, he eventually became a Local Preacher; "his life was good all round and transparent as crystal... It is believed by those who best knew him that he never said an unkind word about nor ever had any difference with any Minister during his long religious life, nor did he love less his lay brethren."[27] Wesleyan Local Preachers find mention in Circuit Quarterly Meeting Minutes. E. Thompson, of Hartley Castle, was a Local Preacher for more than 50 years (29.3.1882), as were Toppin Hall (8.12.1927) and R. J. Todd (18.12.1930). This 1930 Quarterly Meeting also recognised Mr. W. P. Robertson who had "been preaching the gospel for over 60 years." On the copy of the *Kirkby*

Stephen and Appleby Wesleyan Methodist Circuit Plan (1881-1882), on pp. 12 and 13, the Plan reference number for E. Thompson is No. 3, that for Toppin Hall is No. 37, that for R. J. Todd is 50, and that for W. P. Robertson is 27. E. Thompson had represented a long-continuing preaching tradition from at least as early as 1830, as the Wesleyan Plan of that year on page 11 makes clear, his reference number being No. 12. Other Local Preachers are mentioned in the local weekly newspaper, with some indication of their impact on local society. Robert Gate, of Penrith, died in 1866 at the age of 87. "Sixty years ago he had alligned himself with the then persecuted Methodists and soon commenced to Preach the gospel to the poor of the towns and villages nearby and further afield."[28] Mr. Crosby, of Kirkby Thore, died aged 45 in 1889. He was a highly respected Local Preacher in the United Methodist Free Church, as well as being leader of the Band of Hope, honorary clerk to the School Board and treasurer for the village library.[29] Joseph Richardson died in 1929 after more than 30 years' connection with the Wesleyan Chapel at Mallerstang. When nearly 80 years of age he had been received on to the Wesleyan Plan as a Local Preacher; he, too, had been and ardent member of the Band of Hope and a Sunday School teacher for over 30 years.[30] Mr. T. E. Etchell's death was reported in the *Herald* of August 20th, 1932. He had been a Local Preacher, in local government, and Kirkby Thore Headmaster for 42 years. He had helped Kirkby Thore people to make their wills and fill in income tax returns. At Kirkby Thore, he held every Chapel office, including that of Steward and Sunday School Superintendent. John Parkin was a Local Preacher from Appleby. In the front of his diary, or book of Texts,[31] he writes of his visit to North Stainmore, a Sabbath-day's work, on 7.8.1887:

"Got breakfast at nine. Walked to Kirkby Stephen arrived 1.30. Camp Meeting commenced at 2. Got no dinner. Preached . . . Walked a mile to tea. Got my tea at 4.30. Fasted from 9 till 4.30. Then . . . walked home to Appleby, arriving 11.50 p.m. Rather tired, having walked about 24 miles."

He had preached his first Sermon at Appleby on October 4th, 1879. A week later he preached at the Knock Wesleyan Chapel, then, in 1880, he preached at Long Marton, at Brough, Murton Free Church, Blencarn Wesleyan Chapel, Maulds Meaburn Free Church, Dufton Wesleyan Chapel, Knock Wesleyan Chapel, Kirkby Thore Free Church, Murton Free Church, Appleby and Brough. He preached 43 times in the first two years of his preaching, 36 times in the third year and 48 in the fourth year. In 1885 he preached at Crosby Garrett, Winton and Asby Baptist Chapels. His Sermons were generally Biblical and devotional. He gave a lecture on William Clowes at Appleby in May, 1885, which lasted one hour and fifty minutes. He estimated that between 1879 and 1896 he travelled 5103 miles in the course of his preaching, most of which was in the upper Eden valley.

Minutes of a Circuit Local Preachers' Meeting, however, show one outstanding weakness among Local Preachers, common to both Primitives and Wesleyans. This was thought to be a lack of dedication in their calling and, in the second half of the nineteenth century, it was a considerable local and national problem. When the Wesleyan Local Preachers met at Appleby in 1875, they resolved to attend to the matter: "That this meeting having heard with sorrow that many of the brethren have failed to attend to their preaching appointments on the plan and being of that opinion that the interests of God's cause, in this Circuit, cannot be advanced if this neglect continues in the future resolves first, that we as Local Preachers will seek for ourselves a renewed consecration of Spirit body and Soul to the Services of our God second, that in the future we will endeavour to discharge our work on the Plan as in the fear of God. And will not wilfully neglect our appointments."[32] In the Primitive Methodist Magazine (1866) the same concern (at national level) is expressed:

"The cause in many places is being stabbed to the very heart, yea barborously murdered through it. Many societies that were once in a flourishing state are now in the last stages of decline ... and to the neglect of preaching appointments their decay is directly traceable.... These things wring the heart of many a Minister with bitter anguish; they tie his hands, cripple his efforts and paralyse his energies."

Reasons were suggested for this neglect. The Local Preachers, employed in daily hard work, were too tired to prepare for Preaching; or they wanted to be with their families on the Sabbath; or they were exposed to mental depression, bodily afflictions or "Satanic temptations".[33] It could certainly be said that, in the case of farmer-preachers in our area, unforeseen difficulties could arise when awkward cows, milked by hand, or straying sheep, could wreck the Sabbath timetable. How long this undoubted problem dogged the real work of the Kingdom it is difficult to say, though obviously its continuation would seem to be a convincing sign that some of those who were supposed to carry the message were not entirely convinced of its importance. Preachers' meetings, therefore, had to exercise great watchfulness over this problem: a blacker blot when it was experienced in small, isolated places where no other person was able to lead a waiting and disappointed Congregation in proclamation or prayer.

The Gospel was preached, in the upper Eden, by local preachers from the immediate area in chapels made out of stone from the same locality. Many of these chapels are small rectangular buildings with little exterior or interior ornamentation. Spital Chapel (page 14) was characteristic, though it had an interior which could be partitioned for Sunday School. When it was opened in 1865, the religious teaching of children was a Methodist emphasis and the building was called "Primitive School" on the outside. The architectural simplicity is repeated, though with a plain wall cross above the Communion Table, in the new chapel at Brough Sowerby, opened in 1972 to replace a temporary building. (See page 15). Pulpits are usually central (though not at Brough Sowerby) and much more prominent than the Communion Table. The usual musical instrument is the harmonium, still well-suited to the accompaniment of congregational singing in small chapels. In one or two bigger chapels (as at Appleby) there is the luxury of a pipe organ. Like building materials and preachers, the organist also has often had to be 'home-produced'. A fairly common visual aid in Worship is the Pulpit Fall on which is usually embroidered the initials *I.H.S.* meaning "Jesus Saviour of Men" to some and beyond any standard interpretation to others. As with the Quakers, the use of religious symbolism is uncommon, and an obvious Cross, which may remind one Congregation of the love and power of Jesus, may remind another of the Church of England — which could be a distraction in Methodist Worship. Plain simplicity is the chapel characteristic, since there was no point in imitating an architecture which represented a different ritual and doctrine.[34] To have copied the Anglican style in the early days of chapel-building would have been to have lacked Parish sensitivity and to have spent money needlessly. There was, in fact, no money at all for anythging but the plainest structure. So Stephen Brunskill who left Orton to live at Beathwaite Green, near Kendal, describes how he and neighbouring farmers built "a place of our own." He writes "we therefore set about it in earnest and although the people were generally poor, they subscribed what they could cheerfully and farmers in the neigbourhood assisted in carting the materials to the place so that we presently erected a convenient little chapel and settled it upon the conference plan."[35] Not much time appears to have been taken to design a Methodist building which would somehow show both the immanence and transendence of God. If, in Worship, eyes were to be opened, it would be to see the Preacher or the Hymn Book. If they were to be closed, it would be to pray. If there was to be movement, it would only be a few short paces from and to the outside world, temporarily shut out, during Worship, by a brief porch. In a report of the Property Division of the Methodist Church, produced in 1980, one section was entitled "What is the Worship-Room to say?"[36] In contrast, early Methodists believed that revelation by-passed furnishings and architecture and that conversation should be directly and simply between man and God.

It was in house or open-air, however, that preaching was first heard and from which a nucleus of believers grew together through meeting each other, as the Wesleys had required in the 1743 Rules of Society. Since, as John Wesley had also said, "they that do not believe the Bible will believe anything",[37] the importance of Holy Scripture has always been stressed in Eden chapels and Methodist homes. Sunday School Scholars can learn certain passages of the Psalms, by memory, and be presented with a 'Lord Wharton' Bible. Methodism still benefits from the same legacy (willed in 1696), as did the Appleby United Methodist Free Church Circuit, in 1899, when it resolved "that application be made for a Number of Lord Wharton Bibles to be distributed amongst the Sunday Schools of the Circuit."[38] 34 were obtained. The ministry of the Word, read or expounded, was an Ordinance of God which John Wesley's Societies were expected to "attend upon." Unlike the Class Meetings which, even in Wesley's lifetime were not altogether manageable or successful, public and private reading of the Scriptures was always a necessary part of Methodist devotion. So it was a rare and surprising Minute which, in 1842, from Barnard Castle Primitive Methodists, said "that a portion of the sacred Scriptures be read once every Sabbath in all our Chapels and Preaching Rooms."[39]

Leadership problems and the mixing of social classes within the Methodist Class Meeting caused some general decline in its importance during the nineteenth century. From the records we have it is not possible to say that this was the case in the upper Eden valley, since there are so few references of any kind to local Class Meetings. It would be tempting to say that the Wesley Guild, at the end of the century, replaced them, but the aims of the two were quite different. In any case the Guilds, to which we return later, were established when the Methodists had become recognised as the Methodist Church rather than that saintly Society within the Church of England in which John Wesley believed the Class Meeting would have a sanctifying influence.

In the upper Eden valley, in 1885, Class financial contributions were not as forthcoming as they ought to have been. The Quarterly Meeting agreed "that the Secretary communicate with each leader throughout the Circuit, recommending that they make it an invariable rule to regularly collect the Weekly pence in their classes according to Conference rule."[40] Later in the same year (in December, 1885), the Ministers presented their analysis of the Membership in the following way:

"There are 569 members who meet in Class, and pay.
There are 65 members who do not meet in Class, but pay.
There are 40 members who meet in Class, but don't pay.
There are 9 members who neither meet in Class, nor pay.
Total 683"[41]

We note that almost ninety per cent of the Wesleyan Circuit Membership was meeting in Class as late as 1885. But some apparent decline is suggested by remarks made in another branch of local Methodism, when, revealingly, to the Register of the names of the United Methodist Free Church Members in the Appleby Circuit, in 1861, S. Beavan, the Appleby Circuit Minister, added the following:

"I have reported the number of members to the Annual Assembly 1861 as 144 — Because I would make an allowance for some whose names are on Class Books, but whose attendance at Class Meetings of late has been so slight (without any solid reason for absence) as to render them somewhat doubtful."[42] In the Register (1867), however, there is reference to a Primitive Methodist, Isaac Bayliffe[43] of Appleby, who is noted as a Primitive Methodist Local Preacher but who meets in the United Methodist Free Church Monday Class; he does not pay, is a Helper on the United Methodist Free Church Plan but pays to the Primitives. These later Minutes suggest that, in the United Methodist Free Church, Classes were still being held regularly. A Quarterly Meeting at Appleby (21.6.1865) agreed "that Wesley's Rules be read once a quarter in our classes." Barnard Castle Primitive Methodists refer to a possible Class Meeting when they agree "that the fellowship meeting usually held in the Chapel at Barnard Castle on a Saturday evening be held on a Sabbath morning in the stead so as to allow time for cleaning the Chapel etc."[44] Their practical approach is also seen in an earlier rare reference to the Class, in 1844. They agree "that an address be printed containing a plain statement of the present position of the Circuit temporally affectionately requesting all the Members to enter into the regular weekly payment of Class money in order so far to improve the funds of the Circuit so as to employ another Preacher which is so greatly needed."[45]

Local Preachers' Meetings Minutes give only occasional insight to Class Meetings: "Bro Mason have a note requesting him to meet in Class in accordance with our Rule."[46] In 1924 "a discussion took place on forming a Class for the young Local Preachers, and Mr. Rhodes kindly promised to try and arrange a Class at Gaisgill, for the young preachers from Orton, Gaisgill and Ravenstonedale."[47] In 1928, it was agreed that "all preachers be requested to hold a prayer meeting after the night service."[48] This could not have been quite like the old Class Meeting but it kept Methodists together, led by the Preacher and offering prayers to God which may well have expressed the sentiments of those who, in the early Classes, talked to each other.

More important was the work of teaching, especially among the young. Benjamin Ingham's interest in the education of children had been noticeable as early as 1734, when he taught 42 children to read in Ossett; he also taught 12 children on the boat on his way to America with the Wesleys, and when he arrived there in 1736, he spent the first three months teaching children in a school five miles from Savannah where, with the help of two Moravians, he was entirely in charge.[49] In the *Minutes of the Inghamites* for Sunday, April 2nd, 1758 (at Salterforth Chapel, some ten miles north of Burnley in Lancashire), we read:

"At two in the Afternoon the GO" (General Overseer) "kept a Children's Meeting in the Chapel whereat many were present, young and old. And afterwards noticed that there would be one every Sunday after preaching this Summer (rainy days excepted) and that all parents, whether they belonged to us or not, might send their children, if they please."

Eleven years later, John Wesley's friend, Hannah Ball, began her Sunday School in 1769[50] and Wesley's keen interest in her work was expressed in a letter on March 10th, 1782:

"I wanted to know what was become of those little maidens, and trust some of them will bring forth fruit to perfection. As you have a peculiar love for children and a talent for assisting them, see that you stir up the gift of God which is in you. If you gain but one of them in ten, you have a good reward for your labour."[51]

In 1785 he wrote to John Fletcher: "I really hope the Sunday Schools will be productive of great good to the nation. They spread wider and wider, and are likely to reach every part of the kingdom."[52] In 1787 he wrote to Richard Rodda: "It seems to me that these will be one great means of reviving religion throughout the nation. I wonder Satan has not yet sent out some able champion against them."[53] In the same year he wrote to Alexander Suter: "Our Sunday schools at Bolton contain upward of eight hundred children, and are taught by our own brethren WITHOUT PAY. I love Sunday schools much. They have done abundance of good."[54] In 1783 Wesley had expressed his thought on "The Manner of Educating Children" in which were guidelines for teaching: "Does it follow", he asked, "that we ought not to instil true religion into the minds of children as early as possible? Or, rather, that we should do it with all diligence from the very time that reason dawns, laying line upon line, precept upon precept. as soon and as fast as they able to bear it? By all means. Scripture, reason, and experience jointly testify, that, inasmuch as the corruption of nature is earlier than our instructions can be, we should take all pains and care to counteract this corruption as early as possible. The bias of nature is set the wrong way: Education is designed to set it right."[55]

Over half a century later the Primitive Methodists, it seemed, had taken this guidance seriously. Set into the *Quarter Day Account and Minute Book of Brough Branch of the Hull Circuit* (in 1841) we have Sabbath School Regulations. Systematic thoroughness is reflected in the detailed timetable:

"By order of the School Committee August 9th, 1844.
Regulations for Sabbath School.

"Morning. Door to be opened 10 minutes before 9 o'clock. Open School precisely at 9 o'clock. Sing and Pray 10 minutes till 9.10. Read 20 minutes till 9.30. Mark Class Papers 5 minutes till 9.35. Read 20 minutes till 9.55. Spell 5 minutes till 10. Sing, pray and conclude 10 minutes till 10.10. Relieve the children 10 minutes. Have them all seated properly by 10.25.

"Afternoon. Door to be opened twenty minutes past one o'clock. Open school precisely at 1.30. Sing and pray 10 minutes till 1.40. Read 20 minutes till 2. Mark Class Books 5 minutes till 2.5. Spell 10 minutes till 2.15. Read 20 minutes till 2.35. Catechise 10 minutes till 2.45. Lecture 15 minutes till 3. Sing and pray 10 or 15 minutes till 3.10 or 3.15. The children must be kept on their seats till the Congregation has withdrawn. Then the girls must go out first by seniority, the boys in the meantime to be furnished with their hats and caps by their teachers and must not be allowed to seek them themselves. This will prevent much confusion.

"P.S. Each teacher must leave the School at the head of his or her class while the children follow."

Brough Primitive Methodist Sunday School work (in 1844) was only a small part of work on a rapidly-growing wider front. A Wesleyan Conference report in 1837 showed that there were 3,339 Sunday schools and 60,000 teachers for 341,442 scholars. Only a quarter of the preaching places were without a school.[56] A Wesleyan Sunday School had, in fact, opened in Barnard Castle in 1810, "in consequence of great numbers of children being sent at a very early age to the factory, and being thus deprived of the opportunity of obtaining even a secular education . . . the doors of the sanctuary were thrown open ... Scholars came pouring in abundantly, and soon upwards of four hundred names were entered in the books .... Great moral and spiritual good as well as secular benefits resulted from this institution .... The number of scholars it is true, is not so great as formerly, schools of a similar character having since been commenced in connection with the National church, and by dissenting denominations."[57] In 1843 we have reference to Appleby Circuit Wesleyan Methodist Association's children's work. At their Quarterly Meeting in March, at Powis House, near Long Marton, they agreed "that the Revd. Mr. Middleton of Whitehaven be sent for to preach the Appleby Sunday School Anniversary Sermons on Easter Sunday."[58] All the branches of Methodism in our area, however, had Sunday Schools almost as soon as Societies were established. We look, therefore, at various District and Circuit Minutes to observe numbers of scholars and teachers and to attempt some understanding of the relationship between being a scholar and being a Member of the Society. We shall then turn briefly to local newspaper reports of Sunday School work, aware that it is easier to surmise than to prove that being a Sunday School scholar may have isolated that child from young, non-Methodist contemporaries — especially if the scholar later became a Member of the Society and remained loyal to it.

The District Wesleyan Meeting at Whitehaven in May, 1842, says there were 12 Sunday Schools in the Appleby Circuit, with two libraries, 83 teachers and 537 scholars. In 1853, there were 10 Sunday Schools, 425 enrolled scholars and 94 teachers. When the customary business question was asked: "Has the religious oversight of the young especially by the formation of catechumen classes been duly attended to?" the answer was almost as customary: "An oversight has been taken of the young but there are many difficulties in this District to the formation of catechumen classes." There was some reported improvement in the 1856 District meeting: very few catechumen classes but oversight of the young, especially through frequent Sunday School visits by the Brethren (that is, the Travelling Preachers) had "continued thoroughly". In 1865, though Appleby Circuit had 11 Sabbath Schools, 121 teachers and 662 scholars, it did not have any catechumens. Carlisle Circuit then had 30, Penrith 30 and Kendal 42, in a District where there were 6,654 Sunday School scholars. In 1869, regrettably, there were 13 Sunday Schools in the District which were not taken to regular Chapel Services; not surprisingly, Ministers were encouraged to ensure their presence in Worship. By 1875, the total number of scholars in the District was 10,628, an increase of almost 4,000 in one decade. In 1879 there were 15 Sunday Schools (in what had become the Kirkby Stephen Circuit), 152 teachers and 791 scholars. Encouragingly there were then a number of "scholars who (were) members of Society." By 1880 the District heard that some scholars were playing truant — because their teachers were doing the same. In 1881, encouragingly, there were 89 Sunday Schools in which the Wesleyan Catechism was taught. The 1878

Wesleyan Conference, however, had already adopted a plan of Junior Society Classes, "designed to prepare young persons, by Christian instruction and the nurturing of spiritual sensibility, for admission to full Church-membership."[59] The essence of an 1820 Liverpool Conference Minute nevertheless still stood: "We earnestly recommend the uniform and regular practice of catechetical instruction in the families and schools of our Connexion, as being especially important in the present state of our Body, and of the country at large; and we press upon our people the propriety of using our own Catechisms, in preference to all others."[60] In 1838, when the era of undenominational-type Sunday Schools (though frequently taught by Methodists and held on Methodist premises) had begun to pass, Samuel and Robert Jackson (instructed by Conference) prepared a scheme of instruction to help implement the 1820 Conference resolution and the spirit of what Wesley had written in 1756. In Dublin he had "met about a hundren children catechized publicly twice a week. Thomas Walsh began this some months ago, and the fruit of it appears already. What a pity that all our preachers in every place have not the zeal and wisdom to follow his example!"[61]

By May 1889 there were 15,030 scholars in the Carlisle District, meeting on Wesleyan Methodist premises – a figure which had almost trebled in a quarter of a century. In 1894 the importance of the systematic teaching of the Catechism was again stressed and Circuits were required to consider it at their June Quarterly Meetings. By 1900, there were 15,589 scholars in the District but a year later the number had fallen to 15,258, followed by 16,004 in 1905 and down to 11,259 in 1920, when the Kirkby Stephen Circuit had 666 scholars. Six years earlier the local figure had been 985. Interestingly, membership of the Vale of Eden Band of Hope, which included a considerable number of children and young people, was 1,148 in 1905, 967 in 1914 and 570 in 1920.[62] Had the claims of the local Band of Hope (founded in 1873) been as appealing as those of Society Membership? And had Sunday Schools continued as they began at the beginning of the century, "regarded as private enterprises, to be encouraged and assisted, but not to be recognized as part of the machinery of the Church?"[63] The Band of Hope, as we shall see, taught people the wisdom of abstinence from alcohol, while committed Sunday School teaching was about life in *all* its aspects. In 1855, at Appleby, the two Wesleyan Methodist Ministers, Christopher Newton and Peter Prescott, actually complained to the local Methodists that in Warcop Chapel "a Tee-total Sabbath School was taught some time, instead of a Christian Sabbath School."[64]

Local Wesleyan Circuit Quarterly Meeting Minutes, making reference to Sunday Schools and Society Membership gave the impression that, at the end of the nineteenth century, the Sunday School had not, generally speaking, been the gateway into Membership: "Sunday School work not... quite satisfactory at every place, indeed not happening at all in some places",(19.3.1885). There "were Ten Schools in the Circuit not making use of the Catechism ... those schools be Communicated with, urging its adoption", (25.6.1891). "Surprise was expressed that only 20% of our Scholars were found to be Members of the Church, and it was recommended that more careful attention should be given to this phase of our work, and, regarding the Sunday School as a Nursery to the Church, every legitimate effort should be made to bring our elder Scholars into closer fellowship", (23.6.1900). Every "Sunday School in the Circuit be recommended to use the Conference Catechism where this is not already done", (18.6.1904). "While deploring a decrease in the number of Sunday scholars, this meeting is of opinion that in a wide country circuit such as this,[65] the scheme of engaging a paid Sunday School Organiser does not commend itself; and, further, that the money required as the Circuit's quota towards the Organiser's salary could not be raised", (13.6.1918). Numbers of scholars in the Wesleyan Circuit did not vary much between 1920 (666), 1921 (631), 1925 (661), and 1930 (622); these last were in 22 Sunday Schools, with 111 Teachers.[66]

From the Barnard Castle Primitive Methodist Circuit Meeting we find that there were, in 1841, Sunday Schools in Barnard Castle, Brough, Kendal, Staveley and Newbiggin, with 65 teachers and 265 scholars. Here, too, there appears to be the early evident separation between Sunday School and Society: the "Sunday School at Kendal pay 10/-. a year to the Chapel for fire, cleaning and rent", (31.8.1837); the Chapel, nevertheless, oversees Sunday School funds, "£1.7.0. to be taken out of the Sunday School fund at Barnard Castle to purchase hymn books for the children of the said Sunday School", (31.8.1837); the "committee of Barnard Castle Sunday School be allowed to expend their surplus of the School's money to establish a library after supplying the want of the School", (27.8.1839); this "Quarter Day Board strongly recommends books to be given to our Sabbath school children as rewards instead of caps and other wearing apparel at the Anniversaries as heretofore", (19.9.1844); "Barnard Castle Sunday School sermons to be preached Sunday July 19th", (27.3.1846).[67] The Brough Primitive Methodist Branch Minutes say that the Sabbath Schools "be visited once every quarter by the Travelling Preachers", (19.9.1851), and that "there be a Tea meeting for the benefit of Brough Sunday School", (10.12.1852). In the 1887 Primitive Methodist Circuit Report to the District, there were 539 scholars in 1886, 106 teachers and 36 "Catechumen Members"; 323 of the 539 scholars belonged to the Band of Hope.[68] In 1896 some effort to relate Sunday School with Society Membership was probably being made when it was decided "that Mr. Sutton write the Sunday Schools of the Circuit enquiring into the practicability of having a Circuit Examination on 'History of the Connexion'."[69] In 1907, the importance of children knowing about other continents lay in a Circuit endeavour "to hold Juvenile Missionary Meetings in aid of the African Mission fund. . . ."[70] In 1908, either as a result of study of the Bible or of Connexional History, Miss E. Brunskill of Tebay and Mr. Bird of Brough "and the scholars" were to be congratulated "upon the success of the examination. Of the 9 District prizes 5 come to Tebay and one to Brough."[71] In 1912 there was agreement "that Young People's Day be observed, preachers and teachers to direct their effort and appeal towards bringing our young people to decision for Christ on this day."[72] Society Membership could then, but did not always, follow.

As for the smaller Methodist branches, the Appleby Wesleyan Methodist Association Quarterly Meeting agreed, in 1847, that it accept "the offer of ... Bro. Saml. Crosby ... to visit those places in the Circuit where we have a Sabbath School, to address the Scholars and Parents."[73] In 1865, the United Methodist Free Church Quarterly Meeting agreed "that the children of our schools be asked to assist in raising money for the Mission funds."[74] The United Methodist Church Quarterly Meetings say very little about the numbers of their scholars or about any relationship between teaching and Membership. At their 1930 meeting, however, there are 97 scholars who have 24 teachers — an enviable teacher-pupil ratio.[75]

What, we ask, were Eden's Sunday School children actually being taught? In 1866, at Knock Wesleyan Sabbath School's annual meeting, children recited their catechism, together with "scripture pieces and dialogues selected for the occasion."[76] Later in 1866, at Kirkby Stephen Wesleyan Sunday School, children were "publicly examined, reciting Scripture and answering questions on their Catechism; they also recited dialogues and pieces with great credit to themselves and their teachers."[77] In 1868, children at Espland Hill Sunday School Anniversary were examined in Scripture, History and Doctrine by their Teachers; scholars also recited prose and verse.[78] In 1909 certain Sunday School Festivals were held on Good Friday at the Tebay Primitive Chapel, the Appleby United Methodist Chapel, the Appleby Primitive Methodist Chapel, the Murton United Methodist Chape! and the Kirkby Stephen Primitive Methodist Chapel. These were public meetings with visiting speakers. The Appleby Primitive Methodist Good Friday Service was called the "Fruit Banquet".[79] Clearly, we know as little about the actual content of teaching as we do about that of preaching, yet those now long left the sacred classroom would not deny that, as for the children of Jewish families in the Old Testament, the Sunday School teachers were parents to may who knew nothing of God's "words": "You shall teach them to your children, talking of them when you are sitting in your house, and when you are walking by the way, and when you lie down, and when your rise."[80] As with the Jews, the purpose of such teaching was that children should be holy, for God had said "You shall therefore be holy, for I am holy."[81]

As in wider Methodism, the Sacraments of the Lord's Supper and of Infant Baptism were administered in our area, though the few visits of Travelling Preachers meant that these were less frequent than in town and city. Lovefeasts, as elsewhere, declined in importance, even though John Wesley has numerous accounts of them in his Journal, and Benjamin

Ingham (influenced by the Moravians) also conducted such Services. The Barnard Castle Branch of the Hull Primitive Methodist Circuit, however, arranged Lovefeasts at Brough, Mouthlock, and Dufton in 1837, when Collections were 5/10, 5/9, and 1/8, respectively, during the quarter ending August, 1837.[82] Ormside was to have a lovefeast in 1840,[83] a Travelling Preacher not being required. In 1843 the Lovefeast and Sacraments were to be left with the Planmakers who should not fail "to Plan a Sacrament at Mouthlock . . "[84] The Lovefeast took place, in fact, in all the branches of local Methodism but never frequently and never, apparently, as a substitute for the Lord's Supper, even though this Sacrament was not held so frequently as in more-populated places outside the Eden valley. During Lovefeast Services a small piece of cake and water, the elements of a simple meal, were given to all present and taken by them as members of one family united by the love of Christ. The Moravians had believed it to be an imitation of the AGAPE held in the early Christian Church. There is a hint (but it may only be a metaphor from Cana in Galilee) that the Inghamites used wine at their Lovefeasts. "We had our Lovefeast at Thinoaks which began at 8 in the morning. . . . In the conclusion (that is, of the day) we had the Lord's Supper, and the last wine was as sweet and refreshing as the first."[85]

Singing continued as a local Methodist emphasis. It was the most obvious congregational response in Methodist Worship, complementing preaching, teaching and fellowship and also part of Lovefeast and Sacrament. Wesley had given his directions as to how to sing: "Sing ALL, sing LUSTILY, sing MODESTLY, sing IN TIME, and above all, sing SPIRITUALLY."[86] This last he amplified by saying: "Aim at pleasing Him more than yourself, or any other creature. In order to do this, attend strictly to the sense of what you sing; and see that your heart is not carried away with the sound, but offered to God continually: So shall your singing be such as the Lord will approve of here."[87] Singing was, however, only a means to an end, for "that which is of infinitely more moment than the Spirit of Poetry is", said Wesley, "the spirit of piety."[88] Charles Wesley had written the first hymns of the Evangelical Revivial during Whitsuntide, 1738, "when his brother and he were 'filled with the Spirit', and from that time onwards the Methodists have never ceased to sing."[89] The 1933 Methodist Hymn Book had an evangelical emphasis: it contained "a large number of hymns which have proved their power both to deepen the spiritual life of believers and to inspire saving faith in Christ."[90] Charles Wesley wrote 243 of its 984 hymns, though Preachers sometimes tended to choose more hymns by other authors for Congregational singing. This may have been for two reasons: that the music set to Charles Wesley's hymns sometimes tended to be ponderous rather than profound and that the words of other hymn-writers (in simpler musical style) dealt with the feelings of man's religious experience rather than with the attributes and activity of God. Yet Charles Wesley's more popular hymns do speak of the Christian experience and are always Scriptural. At Orton Methodist Church, in fact, in twenty-one Services between November 21st, 1982, and January 30th, 1983, Mrs. H. Alderson (a Member) found a fair proportion of Wesleyan hymns (twenty eight altogether) had been chosen; the sixty one other hymns were by a variety of writers.

Ritson expressed the importance of singing to the Primitive Methodists: "Just as in the Reformation hymns we hear the stern note of conflict, merging into the triumphant strains of an all-conquering faith; or as in Charles Wesley's hymns may be heard the ever-recurring note of a personal religious experience: so in the hymns and tunes with which our fathers carried the evangel through the villages of England, the dominant note of battle and conquest was to be heard. Every hamlet they missioned rang with such martial sentiments as:

" 'I His soldier sure shall be
Happy in Eternity'

and

'Hark, listen to the trumpeters
They sound for volunteers.' "[91]

Primitive Methodists parodied the battle-cry of the Chartists who were themselves beginning to see the importance of open-air work. They chanted:

" 'The Lion of Freedom is come from his den.
We'll rally around him, again and again.'

The Primitives followed this, also in procession, singing:

'For the Lion of Judah shall break every chain
And give us the victory again and again.' "[92]

Mindful of instrumental problems, the Primitive Methodists at Middleton-in-Teesdale, some 12 miles north-east of Brough, could not easily connect fiddle with faith. The Quarterly Meeting, in 1842, agreed that "the singers by introducing the fiddle into the public worship at Middleton without the sanction of the Leaders' Meeting did wrong, tho' they did it innocently; that . . . the Fiddle to be taken from the Chapel . . . and that the Leaders' Meeting appoint a leading singer at Middleton."[93] Six months later the Quarterly Meeting said "that a letter be wrote . . . to the singers at Middleton in the most friendly way possible requesting them to take out the fiddle in the most prudent way."[94] The following May the Quarterly Meeting had to agree "that Brother Sowerby call the Leaders of Mickleton" (near Middleton) "together and state that they must Decide about the Fiddle themselves providing they keep within the limits of rule and a note be wrote to them . . . ." Music and Methodists, ironically, have not always been compatible and it has occasionally been necessary to exercise particular sensitivity in this matter. Sometimes, therefore, it has had to be that the Circuit, rather than the local Church, has advised on procedure, as with the Wesleyan Methodist Associationists in their Quarterly Meeting in 1848, when it was agreed that "a majority is of opinion that an Organ introduced into the tabernacle at Appleby, would be advisable and is recommended."[95] In 1852, the same Quarterly Meeting agreed that it approved "of the Methodistic mode of giving out the Hymns and it would kindly recommend the various societies to adopt that method, that with special reference to Appleby that they be requested to adopt singing as a substitute for their usual manner of chanting."[96] In 1870, the Primitive Methodist Circuit Quarterly Meeting gave Brough Society the "liberty to purchase a harmonium not to exceed £10."[97] This instrument seemed to be culturally suitable here, unlike those which were used by missionaries in India about the same time.

Denis Capstick, once a Methodist farmer at Newbiggin-on-Lune, has some information on particular Methodist singing in the Kirkby Stephen, Appleby and Tebay Circuit. He says a Male-Voice Choir has been in existence for over 25 years, having Sydney Bowman (an Orton Methodist now emigrated to Australia) as its leader in the early days. It has consistently sung in Chapels and in the open-air. "It may well be", he writes, "that this open-air witness of the Choir is its most distinctive contribution to the religious life of the area. We hold open-air services each summer in the various villages and they are marvellously supported – three weeks ago more than a hundred cars were parked on or around the village green in Maulds Meaburn. It is a source of continual surprise to us that the folk in our own locality still want to hear us. Not very long ago we had a twelve month period during which we had invitations from every one of the nine Societies in the Tebay section to share in some special event at each place.... Several (choir) members (at least 25%) are from areas outside the Circuit and we are not all Methodists, we have one Baptist and three Brethren. I think we have sung to audiences of every denomination (except the R.C.) and to those of none .... We have engagements as far away as Pickering (North Yorkshire), Manchester and Glasgow .... We have our own organist ... our organ which we take with us wherever we go ... has been transported thousands of miles. We have approximately 20 in the Choir ... I think all of us would do things for the Choir we would not think of doing for any other organization."[98]

We now turn to events which demonstrated a considerable interest in the world overseas. After the founding of the Wesleyan Missionary Society in 1818, returning Missionaries brought important news back to the homeland. Those who visited the upper Eden, for example, spoke of alarming need, and though our area may not have responded with manpower, it gathered money and said its prayers. The Reverend J. Kilner, returned from Ceylon in 1865 and revealed his bias at Penrith: "I have got a Hindu god in my pocket which three months ago was in the temple and people hazarded their salvation upon it."[99] More agonising was the cry of

Thomas B. Freeman in a letter published in 1844, to the Secretaries of the Wesleyan Missionary Society, regarding the Ashanti:

"When an Ashanti of any distinction dies, several of the deceased's slaves are sacrificed. This horrible custom originates in some shadowy ideas of a future state of existence in which they imagine that those who have departed hence stand in need of food, clothing, etc., as in the present world and that as a vast number of concubines, slaves, etc., are the chief marks of superiority among them here, so it must also be in a future state. Accordingly as I walked out early in the morning I saw the mangled corpse of a poor female slave who had been beheaded during the night lying in the public street. O, Thou God of Mission, who willest not that any should perish but that all should come to the knowledge of the Truth, have mercy upon these benighted people. May Thine everlasting Gospel speedily spread itself through the length and breadth of this land and chase the demon from these his dark abodes of cruelty."[100]

Of West Africa, as a whole, he wrote:

"True, it is a beautiful country. Its fertile soil produces an hundredfold but what avails its beauty or fertility when it is converted into one immense slaughterhouse. O ye who enjoy the high blessings of Christianity allow us to entreat you to direct your energies towards this scene of moral desolation. Brooding in melancholy over the bloodstained wilds, fancy carries me to my native land where entering a well-known place in the Metropolis I hear the cause of Christian Missions advocated, in the presence of thousands whose hearts burn with love towards their perishing fellow-creatures. I hear them speaking of unhappy, degraded Africa, of the pressing wants of its millions, and of the vital importance of increasd exertions on the part of British Christians for the extension of the blessings of Christianity among this mass of immortal men. I hear a resolution moved and supported that much more shall be immediately done for Africa."[101]

The local newspaper, in an array of statistics, takes us in and out of the Eden valley in the nineteenth century. Connexionally, the Primitive Methodist Church had spread, since 1810, to Canada, Australia, Tasmania and New Zealand.[102] In 1861, Milburn Chapel collected £5.13.10 for the Wesleyan Methodists overseas at their annual meeting and £11.12.2 from Overseas Missions collecting boxes and subscriptions.[103] In 1814, Wesleyans had 4 Missionary Stations: West Indies, Nova Scotia, Newfoundland and Ireland. In 1864 there were 605 Stations and 4,618 chapels. In 1814, there were 51 Wesleyan Missionaries; in 1864, 889. In 1814, there were 16,742 Members overseas; in 1864, 142,789.[104] In 1865, the Reverend Frederick Greeves of Bradford proudly pointed out at Penrith that not one Wesleyan Missionary had yet been converted by a Negro or a Zulu. "Fegee" had seen a glorious conversion, firstly, of King and Queen; 20,000 were meeting in Class and 24,000 children in Sunday School and 64,000 regular worshippers. "Missionaries had given these people a code of laws and all this for half the cost of a man-of-war and less than the people of England paid on taxes on dogs."[105] The 'Press' kept the missionary interest alive by reporting, again from Penrith (in 1866) that few Missionaries were in India but "the midnight of that Empire is passed and better days are beginning to dawn." Missionaries were in two Chinese Districts and, in Canton, thousands heard the Gospel every week.[106] At Dufton's annual Missionary meeting it was reported that after 100 years of American Wesleyan Methodism (begun by Philip Embury in 1766), there were some 2 million Members, with 14,000 Travelling Preachers, 15,000 Local Preachers, and 1½ million scholars.[107]

Missionary interest was maintained until well into the twentieth century in our area. Circuit Collections on behalf of Wesleyan Foreign Missions were £105.4.8 in 1894 and £110.12.3 in 1895.[108] In 1897, they were £112.6.0 and in 1898, they were £123.6.8.[109] Then, in 1915, the Wesleyan Superintendent was encouraged by the Quarterly Meeting to assist at Missionary meetings in a neighbouring Circuit.[110] Later that year, the Reverend Harry Haig of Ceylon was to visit the Circuit as a Missionary deputation.[111] In 1919 "the Rev. Arthur W. Turner, who had just returned from missionary work in India, had accepted an invititation to succeed the Rev. E. Ogden as superintendent minister."[112] In 1920, the "Rev. C. W. Garratt read a letter from the Mission House advocating a Self Denial Week for Foreign Missions. It was decided that the suggestion be noted in the Circuit Magazine, and that each society should decide for itself whether to act upon the same."[113] In 1923, the Wesleyan Circuit raised £273.6.4 for foreign missions and £279.0.3 in 1924.[114] In 1927 the total was £270.7.7.[115] At that time there were two Ministers in the Circuit; the Missionary contribution would almost have financed another.

Local Primitive Methodist missionary interest was also considerable and contributions were substantially bigger, in proportion, from the west side of the Pennines. In six months, Dufton Society gave £6.0.0., Milburn gave £8.1.0. and Mouthlock gave £7.14.1½., whereas Barnard Castle Society gave only £5.11.8.[116] The 1844 Primitive Methodist Circuit Quarterly Meeting had concurred "in the missionary regulations issued by the last Conference" and planned to issue as many boxes, books and cards as possible (21.3.1844). In 1915, the Brough Primitive Circuit warmly commended the idea of raising funds for building a Training Institute in Central Africa (3.6.1915). The Wesleyan Methodist Associationists also shared in the missionary interest. "It was ordered that Mr. David Rowland of Liverpool be written to and requested to visit this circuit for the purpose (of) Preaching and holding Missionary Meetings."[117] In 1901 the United Methodist Free Church resolved that two "Baptist Ministers of Kirkby Stephen be asked to serve the Circuit as Missionary Deputations."[118] The United Methodist Church Quarterly Meeting at Bolton in 1930, making arrangements for annual missionary meetings, agreed "that the autumn was really the best time for our Circuit being almost entirely engaged in Farming Pursuits," (11.9.1930). In the widespread and isolated 'mission field' of the Eden valley itself, the interest in overseas work was remarkable, especially when we remember that the financial resources of local Methodism were almost always strained.

It was through the formation of the Wesley Guild in 1896 that some missionary education became more readily available. The Guild, clearly linked to individudal Societies, held regular meetings for devotional, literary and social purposes, and it was aimed, especially, at the interests of young people. Mrs. Metcalfe, a Kirkby Thore Methodist, holds a complete series of programme sessions from 1933 until 1968, when the Guild meetings of the Kirby Thore Society came to an end. The syllabuses contain statements about the purposes of the Guild: "This Card is a token that you belong to a great fellowship. You are invited to help us to make the Guild of real value to our Church and Country and to the world-wide Kingdom of God." On the back of the 1933-1934 session, it says the Guild stands for "comradeship of young Methodists in all lands." Reverend J. E. Ruston conducted a Foreign Missionary Evening during the session. Missionary themes were repeated annually. On November 21st, 1939, the subject was "Burma and Its People"; on November 9th, 1943, it was "In the Steps of Livingstone"; on October 25th, 1944, the Guild meeting concentrated on missionary work in China. From the 1950's, talks tended to become geographical or accounts of holidays in Europe. On January 24th, 1961, an International Youth Conference was the theme. The Quarterly Meeting of the Kirkby Stephen Wesleyan Circuit, in 1914, reported a Guild Membership of 95 at Appleby, 53 at Sedbergh, 25 at Ravenstonedale and 16 at Orton.[119] In 1916, there were three Wesley Guilds in the Circuit, with a total Membership of 184.[120]

The importance of Total Abstinence from alcohol, though not a requirement of Membership of the Methodist Church, was continually stressed in the Eden valley from the middle of the nineteenth century. F. W. Parrott, of Kirkby Stephen, in his Centenary Year Souvenir Brochure (1873-1973) of the Vale of Eden Band of Hope Union, traces the course of a movement which became well established. At the first Demonstration on August 21st, 1873, there was a combined membership of 500 demonstrating against the evils of alcohol. The following year the membership was 982. Nine bands (four brass, and the rest fife and drums) accompanied a procession of 2,000 people in 1876. At the Demonstration of 1919, 3,000 people paid for admission. Brass Bands provided music each year, and singing and sports competitions were part of memorable entertainments. Temperance speakers concentrated on the vital social issue. In 1973, the President of the Vale of Eden Band of Hope Union was a Baptist Minister from Kirkby Stephen. The three Methodist Circuit Travelling Preachers were all Vice-Presidents and Anglicans, too, have also been loyal in their support. The Methodists still give the strongest support to this movement.

From all the emphases we have mentioned in this chapter, personal proclivity prompts one to say that the Methodists seem to have discovered a God who could make a healthier community and a better humanity. Celts,

Catholics and Churchmen had, no doubt, similar convictions but none of their beliefs seem so convincingly documented as are those of Wesley's succession in this other Eden.

---

[1] John Wesley, *The Letters* (London, 1931), III, 229.
[2] John Wesley, *The Works* (London, 1830), VIII, 343.
[3] John Wesley, *The Letters*, VII, 158.
[4] Charles Wesley, in *The Methodist Hymn Book* (London, 1933); hymn 713 (verse 1) and 716 (verse 3).
[5] A. Steele, *Life and Labours of Hodgson Casson* (London, 1854), p. 179.
[6] John Wesley, *The Letters*, VIII, 158, footnote 2.
[7] *Ibid.*, II, 289.
[8] *Ibid.*, II, 137.
[9] *Ibid.*, VI, 134.
[10] *The Methodist Hymn Book*, No. 1, verse 3.
[11] Geoffrey Parrinder, *Religion in Africa* (Penguin Books, Harmondsworth, 1969), p. 65.
[12] *The Methodist Hymn Book*, No. 390, verse 1.
[13] John and Charles Wesley, *The Poetical Works of John and Charles Wesley*, G. Osborn, ed. (London, 1872), XII, 223.
[14] *Ibid.*, III, 149.
[15] A. Steele, *Life and Labours of Hodgson Casson* (London, 1854) pp. 105-106.
[16] John Wesley, *The Journal* (London, 1938), V, 26.
[17] Stephen Brunskill, *The Life of Stephen Brunskill of Orton, 60 Years a Wesleyan Methodist Local Pracher* (London and Kendal, 1837), p. 19.
[18] *Ibid.*, p. 30 (in 1783-1784).
[19] *Ibid.*, p. 21; Martha Thompson had helped to introduce Methodism into York (John Wesley, *The Journal*, IV, 66, footnote 2).
[20] His name appears on the 1830 Wesleyan Plan, page 11, Preacher numbered "4".
[21] R. W. Moss, "Wesleyan Methodism - the last fifty years" in W. J. Townsend, H. B. Workman, and George Eayrs, ed., *A New History of Methodism* (London, 1909), I, 463.
[22] *Plan of the Primitive Methodist Church*, Appleby Branch of the Brough Circuit (January-March, 1922).
[23] W. M. Patterson, *Northern Primitive Methodism* (London, 1909), p. 109.
[24] *Ibid.*, p. 109; that is, Middleton-in-Teesdale.
[25] *Primitive Methodist Magazine* (London, 1866), pp. 620-621; the short biography is signed "J.F.B.".
[26] William Shipley, in *Aldersgate Primitive Methodist Magazine* (London, 1906), p. 494.
[27] *Primitive Methodist Magazine* (London, 1881), pp. 564-566; writer not named.
[28] *Cumberland and Westmorland Advertiser*, 14.8.1866.
[29] *Ibid.*, 26.3.1889.
[30] *Cumberland and Westmorland Herald*, 21.9.1929.
[31] In the possession of his grand-daughter, Mrs. D. Braithwaite, Glen-Eden, Riverside, Kirkby Stephen.
[32] Minutes of the *Kirkby Stephen and Appleby Wesleyan Circuit Local Preachers' Meeting*, 23.9.1875.
[33] *Primitive Methodist Magazine* (London, 1866), pp. 721-725; in an article entitled "Neglect of Preaching Appointments" by "J.M.".
[34] John Wesley described his new Chapel in City Road, London, as "perfectly neat, but not fine." (*The Journal*, VI, 215).
[35] Stephen Brunskill's autobiography, p. 50.
[36] *"So you need a new church do you?"* and *Report of the Trustees for Methodist Church Purposes* (Manchester, 1980), pp. 25-29.
[37] John Wesley, *The Works*, XIII, 370.
[38] Minutes of the *Appleby United Methodist Free Church Circuit Quarterly Meeting*, 15.6.1899.
[39] Minutes of the *Barnard Castle Primitive Methodist Circuit Quarterly Meeting*, 22.12.1842.
[40] Minutes of the *Kirkby Stephen and Appleby Wesleyan Circuit Quarterly Meeting*, 25.6.1885.
[41] *Ibid.*, 24.12.1885.
[42] *The Register of the names of the Members of the Wesleyan Methodist Association in the Appleby Circuit, commencing in 1840, December 21st.*
[43] A railway-worker, then farmer and butcher, he was a strict Sabbath observer. He preached some 2,860 times in 54 years; his son, John, born at Appleby in 1868 became a Primitive Methodist Preacher in 1888 and died in 1950; see Ella K. Crossley, *John B. Bayliffe* (London, 1952).
[44] Minutes of the *Barnard Castle Primitive Methodist Circuit Quarterly* Meetings, 23.3.1843.
[45] *Ibid.*, 21.3.1844.
[46] Minutes of the *Kirkby Stephen and Appleby Wesleyan Circuit Local Preachers' Meeting*, 28.6.1872.
[47] *Ibid.*, 13.3.1924.
[48] *Ibid.*, 1.3.1928.
[49] D. F. Clarke, Benjamin Ingham (1712-1772), M.Phil. thesis, (Leeds University, 1971), p. 182.

[50] John Wesley, *The Letters*, VII, 114, footnote 4.
[51] *Ibid.*, VII, 114.
[52] *Ibid.*, VII, 265.
[53] *Ibid.*, VII, 364.
[54] *Ibid.*, VIII, 23-24; this Bolton is in Lancashire.
[55] John Wesley, *The Works*, XIII, 436.
[56] Cyril J. Davey, *The Methodist Story*, pp. 50-51.
[57] Anthony Steele, *History of Methodism in Barnard Castle and the Principal Places in the Dales Circuit*, pp. 199-201.
[58] Minutes of the *Appleby Wesleyan Methodist Association Circuit Quarterly Meeting*, 21.3.1843.
[59] Henry W. Williams, *The Constitution and Policy of Wesleyan Methodism*, 2nd edition (London, 1882), p. 12.
[60] *Ibid.*, p. 327.
[61] John Wesley, *The Journal*, IV, 157.
[62] Minutes of the *District Wesleyan Meetings* (8.7.1801-May, 1920).
[63] J. R. and A. E. Gregory, "Wesleyan Methodism – The Middle Period", *in A New History of Methodism*, I, 415.
[64] In a *Pastoral Address to the Wesleyan Methodist Societies in the Appleby Circuit*, By the Ministers (Appleby, 1855).
[65] Sedbergh had also been part of the Circuit since 1900, but would be taken from it again in 1919.
[66] Minutes of the *Kirkby Stephen and Appleby Wesleyan Circuit Quarterly Meetings*.
[67] Minutes of the *Barnard Castle Primitive Methodist Circuit Quarterly Meeting*.
[68] Report of the *Brough Primitive Methodist Circuit* to the Carlisle and Whitehaven District, 1887.
[69] Minutes of the *Brough Primitive Methodist Circuit*, 3.12.1896.
[70] *Ibid.*, 9.9.1907.
[71] *Ibid.*, 3.12.1908.
[72] *Ibid.*, 5.9.1912.
[73] Minutes of the *Appleby Wesleyan Methodist Association Circuit Meeting*, 27.12.1847.
[74] *Ibid.*, 21.6.1865.
[75] *Ibid.*, 6.3.1930.
[76] Cumberland and Westmorland Advertiser, 26.6.1866.
[77] *Ibid.*, 8.1.1867.
[78] *Ibid.*, 21.7.1868.
[79] *Ibid.*, 17.4.1909.
[80] Deuteronomy 11, verse 19.
[81] Leviticus 12, verse 45.
[82] *Barnard Castle Branch and Kendal Mission Account*.
[83] Minutes of the *Barnard Castle Primitive Methodist Circuit*, 2.6.1840.
[84] *Ibid.*, 23.3.1843.
[85] Minutes of *The Inghamites*, 30.6.1760.
[86] John Wesley, *The Works*, XIV, 358-359.
[87] *Ibid.*, p. 359.
[88] John Wesley, in the *Methodist Hymn Book* with tunes (London, 1933), p. vi.
[89] Preface of the *Methodist Hymn Book* with tunes, p. iii.
[90] *Ibid.*, p. iv.
[91] Joseph Ritson, *The Romance of Primitive Methodism* (London, 1909), pp. 263-264.
[92] *Ibid.*, p. 271.
[93] Minutes of the *Barnard Castle Primitive Methodist Circuit Quarterly Meeting*, 23.6.1842.
[94] *Ibid.*, 21.12.1842.
[95] Minutes of the *Appleby Wesleyan Methodist Association Circuit Quarterly Meeting*, 28.6.1848.
[96] *Ibid.*, 29.9.1852.
[97] Minutes of the *Brough Primitive Methodist Circuit Quarterly Meeting*, 13.6.1870.
[98] In a letter to me, dated 25.7.1978, from "Brownber", Newbiggin-on-Lune, Kirkby Stephen, Cumbria.
[99] *Cumberland and Westmorland Advertiser*, 2.5.1865.
[100] Thomas B. Freeman, *Journal of Various Visits to the Kingdom of Ashanti, Aku, and Dahomey in Western Africa* by the Reverend Thomas B. Freeman *to promote the objects of the Wesleyan Missionary Society* (London, 1844), pp. 24-25.
[101] *Ibid.*, pp. 49-50; part of a letter written in July, 1839.
[102] *Cumberland and Westmorland Advertiser*, 6.11.1860.
[104] *Ibid.*, 17.12.1861.
[104] *Ibid.*, 5.1.1864.
[105] *Ibid.*, 14.2.1865.
[106] *Ibid.*, 1.5.1866.
[107] *Ibid.*, 27.11.1866.
[108] Minutes of the *Kirkby Stephen and Appleby Wesleyan Circuit Quarterly Meeting*, 23.3.1895.
[109] *Ibid.*, 19.3.1898.
[110] *Ibid.*, 10.6.1915.
[111] *Ibid.*, 18.9.1915.
[112] *Ibid.*, 5.6.1919.
[113] *Ibid.*, 16.12.1920.
[114] *Ibid.*, 12.3.1925.
[115] *Ibid.*, 1.3.1928.
[116] Minutes of the *Barnard Castle Primitive Methodist Circuit Quarterly Meeting*, 25.3.1847.
[117] Minutes of the *Appleby Wesleyan Methodist Association Circuit Quarterly Meeting*, 30.12.1839.
[118] Minutes of the *Appleby United Methodist Free Church Circuit Quarterly Meeting*, 2.12.1901.
[119] Minutes of the *Kirkby Stephen Appleby and Sedbergh Wesleyan Circuit Quarterly Meeting*, 12.3.1914.
[120] *Ibid.*, 16.3.1916.

CHAPTER IV

For a healthier community

In assessing the impact of our holy community, we have to remember that our particular area has not come under the direct influence of what may be called "formidable" preaching. Preachers, for example, like Hugh Price Hughes (1847-1902) of West London did not "Travel" to or often thunder in Eden, where the impetus of preaching was sustained by lesser-known men. Slums and "the working-classes" belonged, with Hughes, to cities. Nor have Eden Methodists been much involved in the stimulation which local Free Church Federal Councils sometimes provide. These Methodists easily outnumber their Free Church brethren and joint-protest to a Government, for example, in a time of national or international crisis, does not as naturally arise as it does in some other parts of the country.

There was also, during the second half of the nineteenth century, the odd (hopefully limited) influence of John Close. Born in 1816 in Swaledale, he later settled in Kirkby Stephen. He called himself Poet Close and wrote critical lines about all kinds of local people, not least local Methodists. He published many "works" and they appear to have had a wide, local interest. Typical of his more scathing attacks, though we cannot be sure how seriously he was taken, were some in *The Wise Man of Stainmore:*[1]

> "From the Wesleyans, with their SANCTIFIED AIRS, as if butter would not melt in their mouths, or sugar dissolve in their tea, you DO expect great things, and are deceived. We rarely ever found ONE Wesleyan that KEPT HIS WORD Sacred . . . . We once employed two Wesleyans to print for us, and both CHEATED us! God's Truth! More of these kind of TRICKS we could unfold . . . . So much for the CONSCIENCE of these Wesleyans: we are almost sick of the NAME! . . . At our Chapel, we are sorry to say that we HAVE SEEN almost every soul of them SOUND ASLEEP during the Sermon; all, excepting the giddy Choir . . . at the conclusion of the Sermon, behold! all the 'Holy Brotherhood' woke up quite lively and chirpy, each heaving a deep sigh and a gentle groan, and look round to see if any SINNERS are affected or converted while they were sleeping. . . . So much for Methodism in 1863."

Wesley who did, indeed, agree that too much sleep "dulls all the nobler affections"[2] would have found equal pen for such adverse comment and we wonder if the Travelling Preacher at Kirkby Stephen stood by his flock, publicly.

What has been the impact of the emphases which we listed in our last Chapter, during two centuries of Methodist work? Statistics, only part of the answer, revealed the following, in 1977,[3] in the Kirkby Stephen, Appleby and Tebay Circuit:

Number of Churches at November 1977	35
Total Circuit Membership at November 1977	724
Total Community Roll[4]	2112
Total Baptisms	13
Total Young People[5]	162
Total Local Preachers at November 1977	40
Total Local Preachers on Trial	7
Deaths	15
New Members	14
New Members from other Circuits	6

The Memberships of the thirty-five separate Societies (totalling 724) were as follows:

Appleby	101	North Stainmore	14
Kirkby Stephen	79	Long Marton	13
Crosby Ravensworth	41	Espland Hill	12
Soulby	35	Milburn	11
Brough Sowerby	34	Bolton	10
Newbiggin-on-Lune	33	Dufton	9
Ravenstonedale	33	Catherine Holme	9
Tebay	32	Bleatarn	8
Brough	31	Spital	8
Kirkby Thore	29	Kings Meaburn	7
Orton	25	Mouthlock	7
Kaber	20	Greenholme	7
Warcop	20	Great Asby	7
Nateby	19	Mallerstang	6
Gaisgill	17	Sandford	5
Winton	16	Maulds Meaburn	4
Crosby Garrett	16	Blencarn	3
		Knock	3

Sunday School Scholars (totalling 307), at 22 of the Socities, were as follows:

Brough	30
Appleby	27
Crosby Ravensworth	23
Kirkby Stephen	19
Blencarn	18
Gaisgill	17
Dufton	16
Newbiggin-on-Lune	16
Kirkby Thore	15
Knock	15
Greenholme	13

Tebay	12
Brough Sowerby	11
Kings Meaburn	11
Warcop	10
Orton	10
Soulby	9
Kaber	9
Milburn	8
Ravenstonedale	6
Mouthlock	6
Nateby	6

Pamela Luke, in her Vice-Presidential Address to the Methodist Conference (June, 1982), listed five present-day difficulties which face, generally, the Rural Church and which, we may agree, are occasionally (sometimes more frequently) experienced in the particular area of our study:

"It is difficult for people to experience real, enriching Worship.

"It is difficult to maintain builings . . . often a strain on resources.

"It is difficult not to develop a siege mentality born out of loyalty, devotion and dogged determination not to close . . .

"It is difficult to attract new members to a small number where any particular age group may be represented by only one or two people and where the majority are likely to be among the elderly. Any sense of mission and outreach is extinct or lies dormant, waiting for an injection of hope to bring it to life again with the conviction that renewal is posssible.

"It is difficult for anyone who has neither been a member of a small church, nor known one intimately, to understand the feelings of those who do belong, who are loyal, who have a deep commitment to Christ, a sense of mission and, who over many years, have received little encouragement either by increase in numbers or by recognition of their position by the Church as a whole."[6]

The population of the upper Eden is now less than it was in 1801 and a description of Brough Primitive Methodism in 1867 would fairly adequately apply to the whole of the present Circuit: "The population of this part of Westmorland is sparse and thinly scattered, consequently overflowing congregations and large accessions to the roll of membership are not in the nature of things to be expected."[7] This assessment had improved a little by 1881 when a Primitive Methodist Minister wrote, of the Brough area, "the dread of change (and) the exclusiveness and suspicion incident to country life existed in no small degree but there were exceptions."[8] A century earlier, the impact of Methodism at Bishop Auckland, in Weardale, (a valley running parallel with the Eden and the Tees), was apparently common to many areas:

"Here, as in most other places, the Methodists were looked upon with suspicion and mistrust. So much so that the people who attended the Services were in the habit of going unobserved whenever it was possible. Happily there was no open persecution but much petty annoyance was inflicted on the congregations when gathered together for worship, such as the letting loose of birds and putting cats and dogs into the room together. Though we are not to do evil that good may come yet in many cases the evil-doers were considerably the gainers as in perpetrating their follies they were brough under the sound of the gospel. Their consciences in not a few instances were smitten by the truths they heard and their scoffing was turned into prayer and praise."[9]

John Colwell, a Wesleyan Minister, compared the roles of Travelling and Local Preachers by describing the itinerant messengers as "comets that moved in high spheres and did not often pass through the orbits of. . . simple villages, but when they did they were treated like comets . . . with great wonder and admiration. Upon the Local Preachers, however, fell the burden of the work and nobly, well and faithfully they did it."[10] Travelling Preachers certainly never stayed long in any Circuit, rarely went back to work in the Circuits from which they began their Preaching, and sometimes, therefore, knew too little about the lives of the people among whom they were sent. Methodist Conferences have tended to think this to be good, though one occasionally wonders how different the impact of Methodist Ministers might have been had they more often "travelled" in the type of Circuit from which they had come in the first place. Since 1950, five farmers' sons have entered the Methodist Ministry from the Kirkby Stephen, Appleby and Tebay Circuit but in 1983, they lived and worked in Houghton-le-Spring and Bishop Auckland (in the more industrial north-east of England), Coventry (in the industrial Midlands), Chorley (near Manchester), and Stoke-on-Trent (in the Potteries). Let the years pass, however, and perhaps these men may be back in remote, rural Circuits – of which Methodism has more than a few.

Local Preachers' Meetings reflect some of the impact of the preaching. "The death of bro. E. Thompson of Kirkby Stephen, the oldest local preacher on the plan was reported to the meeting. Many testimonies were borne of his long connection with the Circuit, the effects of his preaching upon the youth, and the powerful influence of his holy life upon all who knew him."[11] Even John Close wrote of Edmund Thompson, of Hartley Castle, with the highest respect: He "shows an Example worthy of all imitation, so devout and so inwardly engaged in the Holy Worship, becoming all true Christians; but how few are like the THOMPSONS!"[12] The names of both Jonathan and Edmund are printed on the 1830 Wesleyan Plan (Page 11), men from the local community whom Methodism enabled to become leaders for more than half a century. Such preachers were essential to the progress of the movement and in isolated areas, where Travelling Preachers could not often come, these Local Preachers were accepted by Congregations as messengers of God. All they needed was an evident conviction that God wanted them to preach, a readiness to understand and proclaim the Scriptural gospel and a willingness to be appointed to preach wherever and whenever the chief Travelling Preacher should direct. Farmers among them understood, better than most, the New Testament parables about weeds and poor soil, about lost sheep and fruitless vines, and, above all, about new birth. They observed the miracle of growth after winter and they were called to commend a growth of holiness after faith in the risen Christ. They also had the habit, and probably always will, of living on the same farm as long as possible – even when they had reached the age of retirement. So they could well preach, locally, for half a century, during which time at least ten (if not fifteen) Travelling Preachers would come and go. Non-farming Local Preachers, also, tend to stay a lifetime in the upper Eden valley and, on the Preaching Plan (October-December, 1982), there were six Local Preachers who had been preaching for more than 50 years; the farmer among them, George Watson from Raisbeck, Orton (whose son is a Travelling Preacher) became a fully accredited preacher in 1926. His son, Wag Close might have said, is paid to be good – father is good, for nothing. Local Preaching is unpaid.

In order that effective preaching continued, the Chapels had to be built and maintained. Trustees of these various properties have had to furnish and warm the buildings, and these places of Worship have been kept clean and tidy for many years. The impact upon society is hardly architectural, so plain and simple are the buildings, but they are a reminder that, for nearly two centuries, there have been those who did not wish to worship as the Anglicans did and who welcomed others to share in the same kind of Service. A group of Trustees, like Local Preachers, would be formed or renewed from the immediate neighbourhood of believers and would include, as, for example, occupations like those at Gaisgill in 1900: farmer, joiner, shoemaker, grocer, butcher, platelayer and signalman.[13] Part of wider Methodism, this local Trust had to attend to matters sublime and mundane:

"H. Capstick was thanked for past services as Chapel Steward and re-elected. It was proposed by T. S. Sanderson and sec (sic) by J. Beck that Ten Shillings 6 (sic) per year be sent to Headingly College all was agreed. It was also passed that the stove pipe be repaired at the top and also a piece of Sheet Iron be put up behind the stove."[14]

It was also the business of local Trustees to recommend that their particular Chapel might be used as a place for weddings. Thus the Nateby Trustees agreed "that Nateby Wesleyan Chapel be Licensed (sic) for Marriage."[15] Not all chapels were so licensed but those which were demonstrated the Methodist conviction that marriage should be holy and should be seen to be so. Kirkby Stephen Wesleyan Trustees agreed "that the Chapel shall be thoroughly beautiful and that Mr J. Troughton be appointed to see the thing done properly . . . that the Chapel be Licenced (sic) for the celebration of Marriages . . . (and) that the Burial Ground be properly laid out and that the Steward see it done."[16] In the register of *Interments in the Wesleyan Methodist's Cemetery KIRKBY STEPHEN*, the first entry is on 24.5.1843 and the last is one 5.2.1900. Another duty of the Trustees was to ensure that the Congregation could sing as well as they wanted to and this was partly achieved by appointing organists: "Miss Potter is considered efficient to undertake the permanent playing of the Organ and to train and practice (sic) the Choir and if found efficient the Trustees agreed to offer her Six Pounds per Annum . . . ."[17] The Trustees also had to ensure that Methodist doctrine was preached in their buildings though this would have been a difficult duty. There was less than a glimmer of their noble calling in a resolution of 1875, when Kirkby Stephen Trustees agreed that the Minister's Anniversary lecture could be entitled "Crotchety Grumbles in the Church and out of it."[18] Perhaps the Superintendent Minister, who was always the Chairman of Trustees Meetings, proposed the resolution. The Circuit Quarterly Meeting could encourage or discourage local Trustees' decisions and sometimes requested the advice of Conference itself. At other times, the Circuit Quarterly Meeting addressed its opinions to Conference concerning the use of local Trust premises. In 1921, for example, the Kirkby Stephen and Appleby Wesleyan Circuit desired "to place on record its strong objection to the recommendation . . . which proposes to permit the use of Wesleyan Methodist Trust Premises for the ordinary business of Trade Unions. It considers that such use of these premises is outside the purpose for which they were erected, and would be fruitful of grave dissension among the Methodist people."[19] Local Trustees knew that their chapels had been built for preaching and this they had to enable at all times.

The impact of Methodist fellowship, in Class Meeting, Prayer Meeting and Guild, as well as in weekly Worship, was also a new phenomenon in local society. Methodists knew and understood each other in their daily work and non-Methodists expected Methodists not only to be meeting together but also to be setting a holy example. Society also knew that Methodists would bring their beliefs and standards into local government and would want to make pronouncements about what they thought was wrong in society. Methodists, therefore, spoke and acted from a fellowship which gave them its support. Apart from the impact of being seen at regular Worship, local society was to notice, for example, in 1932, the way in which the different branches of Methodism came closer together. This union was only possible because, separately, the branches had learned the value of fellowship, of belonging to one another, of sharing faith and practice.

The strength of the fellowship among the Methodists of the different branches, in the Eden valley, and elsewhere, was tested in the years that led up to Methodist Union. Natural caution finally gave way to moving words and memorable scenes at the representative uniting Service in the Royal Albert Hall in London one autumn afternoon in 1932. The Connexional time-tables which led to this moment began in 1912 when the Wesleyan Conference believed that time had come for a serious approach to the matter of Union. In 1917 a number of leading Wesleyan, Primitive and United Methodists gathered to discuss further steps. In 1920 an outline scheme was presented to the three Methodist Conferences and this was sent for Circuit discussion in 1922. At that time, many Methodists were inclined to think that a movement to union was unnecessary but as the years went by the proportion favouring the idea grew in numbers. In 1925 the Kirkby Stephen and Appleby Wesleyan Quarterly Meeting heard how the Superintendent Minister "had received a letter in favour of all possible steps being taken to foster a spirit of unity and brotherhood among the members of the Methodist Churches involved in the Union scheme. He expressed the opinion that already a fine spirit of unity existed locally, and . . . he did not know what more could be done in that direction. He hoped they would all continue to foster that spirit."[20] In 1929 the possibility of Wesleyan and United Methodists sharing Worship in each other's Chapels at Kirkby Thore was raised in the Wesleyan Circuit Quarterly Meeting,[21] though the United Methodists had considered the idea in 1927. In December, 1929, visiting representatives from the other Methodist Churches . . . received a very hearty welcome." In June, 1930, "Mr. Geo. Watson brought up the question of again having Services at Bretherdale." After discussion it was agreed "that the Secretary write a letter to the Primitive Methodist Quarterly Meeting, and ask if they would have any objection if we held an afternoon Service once a fortnight."[22] Bretherdale, four miles west of Tebay, had had a succession of farmhouse services since about 1862 when John Dinsdale began a Wesleyan Methodist Service in his home. This alternated, on Sunday afternoons, with Greenholme Primitive Worship (three miles to the north-east) which had its own chapel in 1897. John Dinsdale always went four miles beyond Greenholme to Orton Chapel (Wesleyan) for Sunday morning Service on horse-back, if he himself was not preaching. Bretherdale farmhouse Services continued until at least 1923,[23] but the Methodists of the locality were, in spite of the above Quarterly Meeting enquiry, not quite "in favour of again having Services."[24] Such small, isolated Societies had benefited, long before the proposed Union, from this kind of alternating arrangement.

In March, 1931, it was reported at the Wesleyan Quarterly Meeting that "we were co-operating with the Primitive and United Methodists in taking preachers to their appointments and that Whit Sunday would be a special day for exchange of preachers."[25] In June, 1931, the Wesleyan and the United Methodist Quarterly Meetings expressed their mutual desire for organic union of the three local branches of Methodism.[26] At the previous December's United Methodist Quarterly Meeting, the invited Wesleyan Minister said "that though of Different outlook Temprement (sic) etc. the 3 Societies Could be so blended into one that the spirit of the Master would be better revealed to the world."[27] As early as 1923, the Brough Primitive Methodist Circuit Quarterly Meeting had agreed to "see if an arrangement (could) be made to exchange pulpits or hold united services during the next Quarter."[28] In June, 1924, the Primitive Methodists agreed to "plan alternate Sundays at Dufton in connection with the Wesleyan Church."[29] In December, 1924, "a vote was taken on the acceptance or rejection of the suggested basis of union of the three Methodist Churches. There were twenty seven members present, nineteen voted in favour of accepting the scheme and three voted against it."[30] In March, 1931, the Primitives expressed a desire to unite with Wesleyan and United Methodists "in regard to Wesley Day Celebrations on Whit Sunday."[31] This host of positive resolutions, therefore, became a sound basis for the 1932 Union and heralded – to wider society – a deepening fellowship among Methodists of all kinds.

In the 1930's, however, the impact of united Methodism on society seemed no more significant than that of the other Christian denominations. Preaching continued, as did the means for fellowship, but churchgoing was not generally popular. Indeed, when Warcop Methodists celebrated their Centenary in 1972, Miss Agnes Brown, one of the oldest Members, attending the Chapel since 1900, remarked that the biggest change during that time had been the falling off of Congregations.[32] Yet we must not forget the continuing significance of fellowship and the vision of Crosby Ravensworth Methodists, as recently as 1978:

"A particular feature of. . . life in this farming community is the regular monthly farmhouse fellowships. These take place throughout the winter, finish when lambing starts in March or April, and then begin again the autumn. It is a family occasion, when all age groups cram into the room of one of the large old farmhouses in the area for what used to be called a prayer and praise evening. I attended the last farmhouse fellowship for this year at Crosby, where some forty people arranged themselves round the fire against the sub-zero temperature of a hard Cumbrian winter outside . . . . Without any sense of smugness or complacency, the Crosby Ravensworth members recognise the strength of their situation and the great heritage of faith and service that has led to it. As one of them remarked to me: 'We long for people all over the country to have what we have here.' "[33]

This seems more like the original Eden but contrasts sharply with chapel attendance, in autumn 1982, in the 'fellside' villages. Eight people attended Dufton, two attended Long Marton, two attended Milburn and one attended Blencarn. Knock had no Service at all.

The Circuit Schedule (for 1977) showed clearly that none of the 22 Sunday Schools were attended by large numbers of scholars yet, however small, these Sunday Schools gave sacred instruction to the nurseries of the twentieth century Methodist Church. At least, this was the intention of the Wesleyan Conference of 1827: that religious education ought to lead the scholar into the fellowship of the church itself. But "ought to" perhaps suggested a general moral obligation rather than a particular Wesleyan Methodist imperative and one wonders if Methodist Conferences were not strict enough about conditions attached to being on the Sunday School Roll: that, for example, scholars should have had Christian parents who themselves would promise to assist with religious education in the home, for without such background support, Sunday Schools would never achieve the 1827 Conference aim. The aim was right, in 1977, if the teachers were intent that the 307 scholars in the whole Circuit should some day join the Circuit Membership of 724, thus increasing the size of loyal Methodism by almost 50% within a few years.

The Reverend Canon Gervase W. Markham, vicar of three parishes just beyond the western edge of the Kirkby Stephen, Appleby and Tebay Circuit, came to his parishes seventeen years ago. There was then a Methodist Chapel in five of the six villages where he worked. "The Chapels all had one service a week and ran a Sunday School . . . . There was usually a Christmas party, and an Anniversary in the summer, with songs and recitations by the children. These depended on the zeal and patience and loving care of one or two Methodist families in each community. They were enjoyed by the children and supported by their parents . . . ."[34] Mr. Markham thought that the value of such Sunday School work lay, as far as he could see, in the fact that many of the scholars ultimately came to him for Confirmation Classes. If what has happened in his area had been multiplied in the parishes of the upper Eden valley, such an impact would have been noteworthy but if Eden Methodist children had rather become fully committed, as young adults, to the Church to which they already belonged, how much better! This has not been the general rule, however, and most Methodist scholars appear to leave Sunday School in their early teens and then absent themselves from any Church of any kind. In 1893, there were 849 scholars in the Wesleyan Circuit but only 596 Members in the twenty eight Wesleyan Societies .[35] Such Sunday School strength was almost 50% more than the Circuit Membership yet there was no evidence that the number of scholars becoming Members was, even proportionately, more than it is at present when, as we have seen, the Sunday School strength is now but half of the Circuit Membership.

Membership, it seems, grows more from a response to preaching than it does from response to teaching. In 1897, the Wesleyan Circuit had appointed a Mr. Leafe, of Darlington, to be an Evangelist in the Circuit for the month of November and a Mr. Parker of Gateshead for January and February, 1898,[36] and in the Kirkby Stephen and Appleby Wesleyan Methodist *Church Record*[37] (November, 1898) we find there were 669 Members in the Circuit (72 more than in 1893). Evangelism did, however, take place, indirectly, through the Sunday Schools, and, in 1914, the Wesleyan Circuit saw this opportunity, expressed in a Conference resolution that "in each Society a Visiting Band should be formed: that the town village or neighbourhood should be divided into sections and two visitors should be appointed to each section: that the visitors should occasionally visit the houses of non-churchgoers in their section to invite them to our Services, to ask them to send their children to our Sunday Schools and generally to show them that we are interested in their spiritual welfare."[38] There was, however, no further reference to this proposal in subsequent Quarterly Meeting Minutes and, in any case, the numbers of scholars decreased to 661 in 1925[39] and to 622 in 1930.[40]

Local newspaper reports reflected the importance of Sunday Schools. Writing of the Bolton United Methodist Free Church Sunday School Anniversary which had taken place on June 24th, 1860, it said that their Sunday School had a good library which circulated among the children, during the year, upwards of 500 volumes. "Such institutions are a great blessing and speak hopefully for the youth of our land and deserve the warmest sympathies of all parents and the hearty co-operation of every individual interested in the social and the religious progress of the rising generation."[41] On Christmas Day, 1860, Sunday School children "appeared healthy, well-dressed and well-behaved"[42] at Kirkby Thore Bethel Chapel and on Easter Day, 1861, scholars were "well-dressed, neat and clean" at the Tabernacle, Appleby.[43] It was not that Chapel children were children of the wealthy but that Chapel parents were anxious that their children appear at their best in the House of God, even better than someone else's Chapel children. The fact that some of these events took place on great Christian Feast Days might suggest the importance attached to religious education among the Methodists. Clearly, a well-run Sunday School was almost an essential part of village life. At the Ravenstonedale Wesleyan annual tea-party on New Year's Eve, 1866, 90 scholars ate free and more than 50 adults attended a tea party later that same day, in the Chapel. The Committee, which had arranged the Festival, unwisely charged three pence more for tickets than did the Primitives or Independents and few attended. "Last year's more successful Committee will need to be re-appointed – they know better the thinking and customs of Ravenstonedale."[44] The Knock annual Wesleyan tea party took place on New Year's Day, 1867, and the newspaper, as if to acquaint the reader with the true importance of Sabbath teaching, said that 48 scholars were enrolled with an average attendance of 43 and that every child's name in the whole village was on their Sunday School list.[45] A serious approach to education was noted in December, 1899, when in a report on annual prize-giving at Catherine Holme Wesleyan Sunday School, it was said that nearly £100 had "been spent in literature for the perusal of the scholars", since the establishment of a well-attended Sunday School.[46] The newspaper gladly continues to associate Methodist Sunday Schools with what is good in the surrounding society. Reporting on Catherine Holme's 1909 Sunday School Anniversary, it said that many from far and near make an annual pilgrimage to this out-of-the-way, neat and well-kept little chapel, "the inhabitants of the surrounding neighbourhood being proverbial for their hospitality."[47]

A fourth emphasis in the Eden Methodist tradition has been its congregational singing. Methodists do not wish to be silent: apart from small Parish Church choirs and unwilling school-children, they are probably the only people in the area who sing. Yet choirs, like pipe organs, are a luxury and by-pass most of the Chapels. Even so, of few references to Methodist singing in the local newspaper, we read that, on Christmas Day,

1899, at Catherine Holme, "a well-balanced choir was led on the organ by Mr. George Horn",[48] and on July 5th, 1919, an annual Choir Festival was held at Brough Wesleyan Chapel. In most of the Chapels it is the well-played harmonium which leads the singing meaningfully, especially when the organist is familiar with its limited register and the glories of sacred verse. The new Methodist Chapel at Brough Sowerby has a harmonium, in spite of the fact that Connexional advice is against such an instrument. On October 24th, 1982, the appointed Local Preacher, Mr. W. Robinson from Crosby Garrett, chose four hymns different in musical style but the twenty adults (if not the ten children) sang them with apparent sincere and unlaboured adoration. None of the hymns were by Charles Wesley, the last being by John G. Whittier, a Quaker Massachusetts poet, born in 1807.[49] At Orton, on November 14th, 1982, none of the hymns[50] were by Charles Wesley though, again, Whittier wrote one of those chosen, (Number 103). The plain tunes set to the eight Whittier hymns in the *Methodist Hymn Book* deny the type of author he apparently was:

"There was ne'er a man born who had more of the swing Of the true lyric bard and all that kind of thing." [51]

His occasional phrases (for example, suggesting that Christian service is not in "ritual word" and "O Sabbath rest by Galilee! O calm of hills above") point to the Quaker heritage and his local Methodist popularity is born out of the religion of Firbank and Fox, rather than Aldersgate and Wesley.

About a third of the time spent in Sunday worship is devoted to congregational hymn-singing but that, generally speaking, is where the musical expression begins and ends. Organists probably do not have harmoniums at home or, if they do, they do not have time to play them, otherwise the treasures of old, instrumental music (composed by Bach and his predecessors for harpsichord and clavichord) might more often be heard. When we recall that the Wesley Guild, among other things, stood for "Culture of the mind", it is a little surprising that in local syllabuses it is extremely difficult to trace any interest in the use of instrumental music in Sunday worship. On the other hand, a Quaker silence may be more important for those moments of private prayer which precede public worship. In any case, Methodists meet to sing together and listening is nearly always confined to the Word of God and its message. Generally, too, the Congregation (as in other parts of England) comes to Worship 'on time' rather than 'before time', thereby losing the opportunity of contemplation – aided by music or not. We must also remember, as we have seen in the case of the Middleton fiddle, that instruments could be a distraction – especially if they were associated with "the world". Sadly, sometimes conversion itself may have been so self-denying that talents have not always been fully used. Peter Eskholme, born at Whitehaven in 1823, became one of Nidderdale's Wesleyan preachers but, at his conversion, denying himself "of all things likely to impede progress", he decided that his "beloved violin, companion in many a frolicsome hour, (be) resolutely put away, to the disappointment of many in the neighbourhood who had been charmed with its sweet tones."[52] The "frolicsome hours" were probably in a public-house, as an extract concerning the Reverend Hodgson Casson may suggest:

> "He often used eccentric means to excite attention. Passing a public-house one day and seeing a number of youths half-intoxicated within, he entered, a pause ensued, whereon he approached the fiddler and said, 'Can you play the bleeding Lamb?' The startled performer admitted he could not. 'Then I can, I'll sing it', said Casson, and with high rich-toned voice, he sang: 'Christ hath died upon the tree, Glory to the bleeding Lamb.' "[53]

Before we examine the impact of local Bands of Hope and, in the next chapter, of missionary attitudes, we note particular occasions when Eden Methodists have deliberately left their mark on local society. Some of them took bold stands to show what conversion meant to them and though we do not have any account quite like that of Peter Eskholme, in rural Nidderdale (a Yorkshire Dale), other Methodist preachers identified themselves with social righteousness, including, of course, the cause of Temperance. Nevertheless, Eskholme's views were typical in that local people were in no doubt whatsoever about his sincerity. He "declined to retail Tobacco. The sign over his shop once bore the inscription 'Licensed to sell Tea, Coffee, and Tobacco'; but with his own hand he blocked out the word 'Tobacco'; and at the present time many of his books have written in the first page 'Tobacco', indicating that they were bought with tobacco-money, after he gave up smoking."[54]

Though the Eden valley was more rural than the wider England of which Joseph Ritson wrote, we should remember that our area Methodism had direct links with the more distant scene. Travelling and other visiting preachers had found that converts all over the country had ways of leaving their mark: sometimes as groups, and sometimes, like Eskholme, as individuals. "It was in rural England that the great work of Primitive Methodism was done. When machine-breaking, incendiarism and violence were rampant, when secret drilling and open riot were prevalent, it came as a healing and regenerative force creating innumerable centres of sweetness and light. If it inculcated principles of freedom and independence, it laid equal emphasis on obedience to the Law, everywhere discouraging violent remedies for the removal of grievances. While in no sense a political Church, it prepared men for the intelligent discussion of political questions and gave them the instincts which must constitute the foundation of a wise and stable democracy."[55] There were other ways, too, in which Methodist conviction was expressed. Mr. Westmorland, a Wesleyan Methodist in the Kirkby Stephen and Appleby Circuit, was appointed a Magistrate "for the welfare of the Community in the County of Westmorland."[56] A Petition on behalf of the Sunday Closing Bill (for Ireland) was brought to the Wesleyan Quarterly Meeting at Kirkby Stephen in 1898, and "the Chairman was directed to sign the same on behalf of the Meeting.[57] In 1902 the Wesleyan Quarterly Meeting condemned "the Education Bill now before Parliament, as being retrograde in the interests of Education and unjust to Nonconformity by providing out of Public Funds for Sectarian teaching without representation."[58] The following year it urged upon the Prime Minister and the local Member of Parliament the need for the more effective control of the Liquor traffic and encouraged "all friends of Temperance to exert themselves to prevent the passing" of the wrong kind of legislation.[59] In 1908 the Circuit gave strong approval to the Government for the introduction of a Licensing Bill.[60] In 1912, Brough Primitive Methodist Circuit urged the Government to make its 1908 promise legal.[61] The Wesleyan Quarterly Meeting at Warcop, in June 1923, unanimously urged the Government to "grant facilities for the speedy passing into law of Lady Astor's Bill, and, further . . . not to give official sanction to the evil of betting."[62] In further consideration of the purity of the life of the nation, local Methodists from the Quarterly Meeting sent the following resolution to the Prime Minister and to the Member of Parliament for Westmorland:

> ". . . this meeting representing 27 Churches and 22 Sunday Schools hereby calls the attention of His Majesty's Government to the great encouragement to the evil of gambling by the development of greyhound racing, and asks for legislation to protect the moral life of young people, and the National well-being of the Country."[63]

Two years later the Quarterly Meeting "desired to express their disapproval of any proposed attempt by hospital authorities or charitable institutions to raise necessary finance by means of sweepstakes or lotteries of any description."[64] Carried unanimously was a resolution in 1931 which opposed the repeal of the Act of 1781 "unless satisfactory proposals protecting Sunday from commercialisation and secularization are put in its place. We believe that the maintenance of the Christian Sunday as pre-eminently the people's rest day is essential to the highest good of the people and that the legislation of Sunday Entertainments is against the best interests of the Nation."[65] The United Methodist Free Church was also involved in protest by petition and in 1904, at their Appleby Circuit Quarterly Meeting, they "resolved that (a) petition be sent to Mr. R. Rigg, M.P., for presentation to Parliament against the proposed legislation for the restriction of Magisterial discretion in regard to the renewing of licences to public Houses and against the importation of Chinese labour into South Africa."[66] Some of these resolutions may have been suggested by Connexional Committees or their wording may have been the handiwork of local Superintendent Ministers, but the fact that local Methodists obviously gave the various matters serious consideration points to a holy community which was not satisfied with the social purity of the Nation.

Apart from alcohol abuse, which we will look at later, there were other issues on which Methodists spoke and acted. After sermons preached by the Reverend Spettigue on behalf of the Lancashire cotton operatives in the United Methodist Free Church at Appleby, Collections were taken to meet their distress. At Kirkby Thore Bethel Chapel a liberal Collection was also taken.[67] The Vicar of Appleby (the Reverend Mr. Milner) made a further appeal and the Appleby Wesleyan and United Methodist Free Church sent considerable sums within a few days.[68] In 1866, the Nation's cattle were attacked by Rinderpest and the President of the Wesleyan Conference wrote to Superintendent Ministers requesting them to arrange public meetings for prayer and to preach with special reference to the Plague. The local newspaper noted this request on 27.2.1866 and a week later a correspondent noted, with appreciation, this Wesleyan Day of Prayer and he invited brother-Christians to pray that "this terrible calamity" might be turned away from the land.[69] By the end of the year most of the cattle plague had disappeared and the County was declared disease-free in April, 1867.[70] Westmorland was spared the bovine ravage, either because the Methodists prayed or because her borders with Yorkshire, on Stainmore, were carefully watched. Gypsies and tinkers were disinfected on their way into the County and cartwheels were scraped and sponged. The newspaper reported that the very earthly Duke of Hamilton's Ayrshires were "said to be enjoying a clean bill of health down his coal shafts."[71]

The Kirkby Stephen, Appleby and Tebay Circuit Quarterly Meeting in 1942, representing 1, 176 Circuit Members, protested to its own Conference that it should have recently permitted (under certain conditions) dancing and card-playing on Methodist premises.[72] As with so many of its protests, we cannot be sure how useful they were, but local society was not allowed to forget that Eden Methodists existed and should be given a hearing. Three quarters of a century earlier, (surprisingly), the Appleby Wesleyans had held their Bazaar in the King's Head Assembly Room on three days in August 1867 and it had become the scene of what many fellow-Methodists might have described as a minor gamble: "While the ladies were busily engaged in disposing of their tasteful wares, others were also helping forward the work in hand. Some in promoting "raffles" for the more valuable articles; others in inducing you to try your luck at the bran tub 'Every draw a prize.' "[73] The fact that such an event was not on Wesleyan premises made it no less contrary to Wesleyan principles. Interestingly, the Inghamites, like the Moravians, drew lots – but only to discover what was the will of God.

Office-holders and Preachers in the Circuits had, of course, to evidence holiness in their own lives. Miles Moss, for example, began as a Primitive Methodist Travelling Preacher in 1833. He was not in debt, did not smoke, and was a "peaceable man".[74] On the other hand, F. N. Jersey was a Travelling Preacher turned Baptist. "When he came into the Circuit he proposed himself Missionary Treasurer and when we came to balance accounts the Circuit wanted £7/0/11¾. He positively declared that he was insolvent and had nothing to pay us with although on the Quarter Day he asserted he was out of debt. We have succeeded after much trouble to get him to give us a promisary (sic) note upon stamp for £7.0.0 to be paid within

6 months by 2 instalments. . . . [75] James Stolbert, of the Kendal Mission, ceased to be a Primitive Methodist Member in 1843. He was guilty of immoral conduct and went away suddenly, leaving debts to the amount of several pounds unpaid and made no arrangement for their repayment.[76] At the preacher's Meeting at Barnard Castle in 1847, William Collinson was "requested to attend a special committee meeting for the examination of certain charges preferred against him . . . . If W. Collinson should . . . decline attending a committee meeting or find it impracticable so to do, then should he still consider it his duty to obey his Master's commands in deference to horse-racing, foot coursing and various other vanities lately carried on at his house, he be respectively desired to yield up his office as Class Leader in Lunedale."[77] Circumstances later showed that he was not entirely at fault, though horse-racing was still wrong: "Brother W. Collinson was in fault when he attended the races at the command of his employer, (but) considering the extenuating circumstances he relates and his promise to be careful for the future he (is) exonerated from blame and . . . it (is) the opinion of this meeting that to attend horse-racing is sinful in the sight of God."[78]

Apart from the missionary emphasis, Methodist concern for scriptural holiness and human need in the immediate locality also reached overseas. Local Circuit Wesleyan Minutes from 1871 onwards show this extended care. In 1871, the whole Circuit agreed, at Warcop, to make a Collection "in behalf of Methodism in France, in order to relieve its sufferings in connection with the recent war",[79] as it did to aid Indian famine victims in 1877.[80] Its further concern for India was seen in 1889 when it urged Government to enforce its 1888 Act "forbidding the Continuance of licensed prostitution, in Connection with the Military establishments of India."[81] In 1896, Eden valley Methodists turned their attention to the Turks:

> " . . . this meeting expressing its horror and indignation at the terrible and Continual Massacres of Armenians Under Turkish rule, calls upon Her Majesty's Government to take immediate and effective measures for bringing to an end the reign of terror which has so long disgraced the Civilized World, and for Securing to the Christian, and all other subjects of the Turkish Empire, freedom from persecution, and safety of life and property, and that a copy of this Resolution be sent to the Prime Minister, and to the Member of Parliament for the Northern Division of Westmorland."[82]

In 1900, Indian famine was again to be relieved from special Circuit Collections.[83] In 1904, a protest was made against the 'Chinese Labour Ordinance', declaring that "inasmuch as whatever are the Economic reasons adduced in favour of such an Ordinance, indentured labour as therein set forth is subversive of moral principle and opposed to the best traditions of the British Nation."[84] In all these resolutions, local Methodism was becoming a little more aware of a world of politics and need beyond the surrounding fells, and with this consciousness was, as we have seen, a missionary interest – also common to wider Methodism and to other

Christian Churches. This considerable holy concern for people far away was matched, if not surpassed, by an evident desire that people, especially children and young people here in the Eden valley, should, almost above all else, it sometimes seemed, abstain from alcohol.

Joseph Livesey had pioneered Temperance education among the young. Born at Walton, near Preston, in 1794, he lived his boyhood days in a miserable cottage at the unprofitable occupation of weaving. All around him was excessive drinking. On March 22nd, 1832, therefore, he founded the Preston Temperance Society, the Pledge required of its members being a promise not to drink spirits. Joined by six other men later in 1832, Livesey signed the total abstinence pledge. Their example was followed in many towns and villages all over England, including Birmingham and London. Another worker in this new movement was Mrs. Ann Jane Carlile, born Ann Jane Hammil in 1775 in a little village in County Monaghan, Ireland – a country where alcohol is not unknown. She came over to Scotland and England to proclaim Temperance, having first formed a Temperance Society in Dublin, among sailors. On her third visit to England, she met the Reverend Jabez Tunniclifff, a young Baptist Minister, who, in 1842, had become Pastor at South Parade Baptist Church in Leeds and who had persuaded the Leeds Temperance Society to invite this Irish Presbyterian Minister's widow to address it on the evils of drink. Speaking at one of the childrens' meetings, she addressed it as a "Band of Hope" and, on November 9th, 1847, the first Band of Hope Festival was held in South Parade Chapel Schoolroom.

The impact of this emphasis was publicly recognized by the beginning of this century. Already, 3,000 children and 1,000 adults had attended the first National Band of Hope Union Festival in the Crystal Palace in 1856. This non-denominational movement was beginning to influence the welfare of the Nation's children towards the end of the Victorian era. At the turn of the century, Liberals were able (supported by Nonconformists against the brewing industry) to introduce drink legislation which, as we have seen, was encouraged by local Methodists in the Eden valley. In 1886, however, though Parliament had forbidden the sale of liquor to children under 13 years of age for consumption on the premises, there was still much to be accomplished by Temperance work and it was in this context that Methodists in the Vale of Eden saw the need to continue their programme against alcohol abuse.

By 1933, Sir Edgar Sanders, Director of the Brewers' Society, was alarmed that the chief customers of public-houses were elderly and middle-aged men. In his eagerness to see the brewing industry steady on its feet, he urged fellow-brewers to instigate campaigns which would bring back young people into the public-houses, especially those who, as yet, did not know the taste of beer. He encouraged Press advertising, though, with appeal to a certain section of the community, this had been fashionable as early as 1866. In that year of the cattle plague, the fairly prominent front-page advertisement in the *Cumberland and Westmorland Advertiser* read, in part, thus:

> "European and Colonial Wine Company . . . for the purpose of supplying the nobility, gentry and private families with pure wines of the highest character at a saving of at least 30%."[85]

In that year, Mr. J. Sarjent, A Temperance agent, had spoken at Bampton (near Shap), comparing Rinderpest and the drink pest. Both would be got rid of by legislative measures.[86] In the case of the latter, these measures tarried, but by 1933 had been to some extent effective - hence Edgar Sanders' concern that England should be a land fit for brewers to live in. His campaign was successful and the Second World War did nothing to encourage Temperance. By 1946, the Band of Hope, therefore, had a considerable task, not least that of educating schools and Churches as to the continuing dangers of alcohol.

Distinctive social emphases , however, were bound to isolate Methodists from fellow-workers and sometimes from relatives, especially if the relatives did not understand how much these new forms of social behaviour were important to those who practised them. Yet this was, and still is, the required aim of all Methodist Churches (as it was Wesley's): to spread Scriptural holiness throughout the land. Even before his conversion, John Wesley knew the need if he did not know the means of meeting it. So he wrote to his father, in 1734:

> "There is scarce any way of doing good to our fellow creatures for which here is not daily occasion . . . here are poor families to be relieved; here are children to be educated; here are workhouses wherein both young and old want, and gladly receive, the word of exhortation; here are prisons to be visited, wherein alone is a complication of all human wants; and, lastly, here are the schools of the prophets - here are tender minds to be formed and strengthened, and babes in Christ to be instructed and perfected in all useful learning."[87]

As for buying or selling spirituous liquors, or drinking them, only extreme necessity, the two brothers said in 1743, should prompt such behaviour.[88] In all this, John Wesley had to point out that he was not commending a new type of Christianity but only "the plain, old Christianity that I teach, renouncing and detesting all other marks of distinction."[89] In describing the character of a Methodist, he writes: "Whether he sit in his house or walk by the way, whether he lie down or rise up, he is promoting, in all he speaks or does, the one business of his life; whether he put on his apparel, or labour, or eat and drink, or divert himself from too wasting labour, it all tends to advance the glory of God, by peace and good-will among men."[90]

We read the local newspaper on the subject of abstinence from alcohol, aware that it took considerable notice of the Band of Hope and the other related movements. From 1860, we trace, in its columns, the caue of Temperance as it makes its impact on local society, remembering that the abstinence movement, though considerably supported in the Eden valley, was also a national campaign against a national evil. It would have been inappropriate, even if desirable, for local Methodists to have opted out of a fight against an evil whose most damaging effects, numerically, nevertheless, were more probably in Bermondsey than in Brough.

In March, 1860, the Kirkby Stephen Temperance Band visited the new Chapel at Asby (opened the previous year) where a temperance plea was loudly made regarding what was called the "Nation's curse."[91] Murton Chapel, also managed by the United Methodist Free Church, held its annual Temperance Festival on Good Friday, 1860. The Reverend Beavan, their Travelling Preacher, lectured in the afternoon and a Doctor Blades from Kirkby Stephen spoke about the evils of drink in the evening.[92] In May 1860, the annual Temperance demonstration was held at Kirkby Stephen. The whole town, all 1,339 of it, seemed to be involved. Flags and banners had been placed on prominent windows in the town and on the lofty Temperance Hall, built so soon (1856) after the first such building at Bradford in 1851. There was a holiday spirit, with many visitors in the town, including the Bainbridge Brass Band from Wensleydale. The procession from the Temperance Hall, headed by the "splendid silk flag", showed David slaying Goliath. At the Tea party some thousand people drank "the cheering but unintoxicating cup." Doctor Blades chaired the Public Meeting at which F. R. Lees, another doctor, gave a Temperance Address. This "great North of England Temperance Demonstration" also witnessed the ascent of a balloon - in honour of the Band of Hope - "materials for which were given and the workmanship executed by working men."[93] As month followed month, the "cause" dominated the social scene. In June 1860, Anglicans joined Methodists to hear Doctor Close, Dean of Carlisle, speak on Temperance at Appleby in the British School; present were the Rural Dean, the Reverend E. Heelis (from Long Marton), the Reverend J. Milner (from Appleby), the Reverend T. Clarke (from Ormside), and the Reverend John Heelis (also from Long Marton). In addition there were the Reverends Brown and Beavan, Wesleyan and United Methodist Free Church Ministers respectively. Doctor Close's concluding argument, much heard since, was that "the moderate drinker did more to promote drunkenness than the real drunkard because they made drinking look respectable and they did not know how many they had unconsciously been the means of leading astray."[94]

In February, 1862, a public Temperance meeting was held in the National Schoolroom at Long Marton, addressed by Mr. Thomas Worsnop from Bradford. The audience included "a large company of the working classes", several of whom signed the Pledge.[95] The Northern Temperance League had 123 affiliated Societies in Cumberland, Northumberland, North Yorkshire and Durham and Mr. T. J. Dryden was the local correspondent, living at Renwick.[96] The League provided speakers and, as a 'leagued' association, it allowed bigger groups in towns and cities to share the costs of reaching the small rural communities. It could enter into negotiations with Parliament and help isolated causes to present, together, with one voice and at one time, their particular views on Law reform. Every League official did his work free and, by 1862, one of its representatives had been to Milburn.[97] The Kirkby Stephen annual Temperance Festival was much assisted, in 1862, by the new Eden Valley railway line. Nearly 500 souls left the Station "when their carriages had discharged their human freight."[98] In the same year, a Mr. Lapsley spoke in the Brough Temperance Hall and Brough joined the Temperance League. Lapsley also lectured, "about that time", at Appleby, Asby, Warcop and Milburn, places where 'Leagued' societies were also formed.[99] In June 1862, Lapsley visited Bolton Wesleyans who became affiliated to the Temperance League, bringing to 16 the number of Temperance Societies in the area.[100]Later in 1862, Doctor Close commended the Temperance Movement to ladies. As for poverty in Lancashire, he thought much of that could have been put right if drink had been left alone. Clergy and gentry, too, if they could give the amount of their annual drinking bills to starving people, would do much for this necessary relief of the working classes.[101] A practical step was suggested by Mr. G. McCree, secretary of the Band of Hope Union in London, who appealed for happy well-fed children belonging to the Union to give some coin for the poor, hungry weeping children of the cotton counties.[102] In May 1863, George Dodds from Newcastle spoke at Kirkby Stephen Temperance Festival, saying that abstainers never substituted their views from the Gospel but sometimes abstinence was the first step to believing in the Gospel.[103] In 1864, the newspaper reported that a total abstinence association had just been formed among the young men of the University of Oxford, purely from a wish to mark their recognition of, and to identify themselves with, this great national movement.[104] In 1865 the Kirkby Thore open-air Temperance Festival was held "in celebration of the closing of one of the four public houses in the village, the Oddfellows Arms, through the purchase of the property by Mr. Thomas Westmorland of Penrith, an ardent friend of the Temperance and Prohibition Movements."[105] In February 1867, Appleby Band of Hope members gave entertainment in aid of their funds in the British School-room. Over seventy youngsters took part and one adult gave a special donation of a Sovereign.[106] A year later "in the House of Commons . . . petitions were presented by Mr. W. Lowther from Ambleside, Dufton, Knock and Great Asby in favour of the Bill for prohibiting the sale of intoxicating liquors on Sundays.'[107] In June 1868, the ancient Ravenstonedale Pot Fair took place on the same day as the Temperance Festival, both thus being well attended. Brough Brass Band accompanied flags and banners and "between two and three hundred partook of an excellent tea" in the Independent Chapel.[108] Winton Baptists took up the Temperance cause in November, 1868.[109] Eleven years later, the Vale of Eden Band of Hope Union reported, at Appleby, that it had 27 Bands of Hope, with 2,507 members.[110]

Temperance work continued through both the Northern Temperance

League and the Band of Hope, the early Temperance Movement being independent of Methodism in that it built its own Temperance Halls. Anglicans continued their interest and in January 1889, the Reverend John Heelis chaired the annual Temperance meeting in the Kirkby Thore Board School.[111] Nateby's Band of Hope appeared to be thriving in February, 1889,[112] as did Crosby Garrett's, which had a monthly meeting in the Baptist Schoolroom.[113] Bolton's Band of Hope was held in the Free Methodist Chapel in March, 1889;[114] Orton's Band of Hope met in its Temperance Hall during the same period.[115] Later that year the seventeenth annual Demonstration of the Vale of Eden Band of Hope Union took place at Kirkby Stephen, when it was reported that almost every village in the Dale possessed its Band of Hope. In less than two decades 39 Bands of Hope had been started and their total membership was 3,678; 411 meetings had been held during the year 1888/1889 and 232 had signed the Pledge. The Railway Companies provided special Demonstration trains in 1889, with cheap fares. There were four Brass Bands and a procession of more than 3,000 children, wearing their membership badges. Kirkby Stephen Wesleyans and Primitives were represented, as were the villages of Crosby Garrett, Winton, Orton, Musgrave, Kirkby Thore, Nateby, Tebay, Milburn, Soulby, Warcop, Colby, Asby, Bolton, Ravenstonedale, Blencarn, Appleby, Brough, Mallerstand, Dufton, Hilton and Murton, Espland Hill and Knock. They all petitioned Parliament in favour of Sunday closing.[116] By 1899, Kings Meaburn, Hoff and Long Marton had been added to the list of villages represented at the Demonstration.[117]

The weekly *Herald* quoted a Doctor Saleeby in 1909, who, it was said, would deny the rights of parentage to people given to excessive drinking. This eminent sociologist had told the Eugenics Society that alcoholism was responsible for producing a defective race and science could prove it. Future legislation would have to be radical and ban parentage to either sex and of any social status who were drunkards.[118] Such legislation would increase the numbers of bachelors and spinsters in Kirkby Thore's population of 427 where were those surely and quickly qualifying in a village which had at least 12 licensed houses in its area. The area of Hilton was even more "under the influence": its population was 120 and it had 7 licensed houses.[119] On one side of the opposing armies were 44 Bands of Hope and on the other was this thick spread of taverns. In the middle were people like Mr. Moordaff, an Appleby Solicitor who had been found guilty of fraud. Counsel at the Assizes spoke of this 'most lamentable case' being the painful story of a drink-ruined family.[120] The Band of Hope and the Temperance Movement had come into existence to prevent such stories and we wonder what society might have become had not their influences been brought to bear on this social evil.

The yearly Demonstrations lapsed during the War years but they were to be resumed in June, 1919.[121] When, in 1929, a "tablet" was unveiled in Leeds in memory of the founder of the Band of Hope, the national membership was over two millions in 15,000 societies. The *Herald* reported the event, quoting the inscription on the building on Leeds Bridge which said that the Band of Hope was a title suggested by the Reverend Jabes Tunnicliff, a prominent Leeds Temperance worker.[122] The local newspaper also gave a significant account of an early Pledge-signing in May, 1932; though without date, it appears to refer to a time, a century earlier, soon after the Preston men signed their Pledges on the first of September, 1832. At Blackburn, Thomas Whitakker and his brother William signed the Pledge at a large meeting in the Theatre Royal. Thomas then asked his employer if his wages could be paid at the mill instead of at the public house. His employer agreed but his workmates, who thought he was slighting them, objected. Thomas Whitakker could not abandon total abstinence and so he left his employment. He became a Temperance Missionary, a Justice of the Peace and Mayor of Scarborough. His son, Sir T. H. Whitakker, M.P., was known to all social reformers. Through a visit to Aspatria, Thomas Whitakker "converted" Sir Wildred Lawson and his entire household. They all signed the Pledge. One son, another Sir Wilfred Lawson, became the popular and long-serving President of the Temperance Alliance.[123]

During the Second World War, when the Vale of Eden Band of Hope was planning winter activities for its session 1942-1943, it sent a message of good cheer to all former members then serving in the Forces.[124] In July 1952, the Reverend B. L. Simpson, Methodist Minister at Appleby, and J. C. Salkeld (also a Methodist) disapproved strongly of the application for a licence to sell drink in the Appleby Public Hall. At the Court hearing, the Police also disapproved and the application was not granted.[125] At the 83rd (1962) annual Demonstration, Anne Hastwell of Kaber, successfully examined in the Vale of Eden Temperance examination, was presented with a cup for the highest marks. Thirty-two Bands of Hope were present and the work of the Union seemed to be remaining strong.[126] But in 1972 there were only 17 Banners and, apparently, there should have been 38. In the previous five years, numbers of people attending had declined considerably.[127] Thomas Hodgson, editor of the local newspaper from 1860 to 1913, together with the succession of Tom Sarginson (1913-1951), Robert Irving (1951-1952), George Hobley (1952-1963) and Frank Shaw (1963 onwards)[128] had all done their best to report the rise and fall of the Band of Hope, and in an age of continuing advertisement by brewers, the impetus of the movement had slowed down considerably, even though it was, by no means, without relevance.

The aims of the Band of Hope have been so much linked with local Methodism that the existence of one may seem to be directly dependent on the existence of the other. When we note present statistics, therefore, revealing a gradual but certain decline in Methodism as well as a similar state in the Band of Hope, we fear for the continuing Methodist identity.

We wonder if some religious groups have only survived because they demonstrated particular SOCIAL emphases. If one of these emphases weakens (especially if it has been the most distinctive), may it not be that the rest are also doomed? This is a relevant question for those whose social priorities become more dominant than their religious beliefs, since total abstinence, nuclear disarmament, or caring for the environment, can never, *of themselves,* be anything but a very significant humanitarianism.

---

[1] John Close, *The Wise Man of Stainmore* (Kirkby Stephen, 1864), pp. 111-116.

[2] John Wesley, *The Letters*, VII, 75.

[3] The last available Connexional Membership Returns (1976-1977), being a summary of the *Circuit Schedule.*

[4] This total includes baptized children, children in family Church or Sunday School and adolescent or adult adherents as well as full members.

[5] This total includes the 13-26 age group under Methodist auspices, for example, Methodist Youth Fellowships or young people at regular coffee bars, discotheques or youth centres.

[6] *Methodist Recorder*, 1.7.1982, p. 18.

[7] *The Primitive Methodist Magazine* (London, 1867), p. 559 (in an article by "J.F.B.").

[8] *Ibid.*, 1881, pp. 376-377 (in an article by Mr. Clemitson).

[9] Matthew Braithwaite, *History of Wesleyan Methodism in the Bishop Auckland Circuit* (Bishop Auckland, 1885), pp. 20-21.

[10] John Colwell, *Sketches of Village Methodism* (London, 1877), pp. 12-13.

[11] Minutes of the *Kirkby Stephen and Appleby Wesleyan Local Preachers Meeting*, 29.3.1882.

[12] John Close, *The Wise Man of Stainmore*, p. 116.

[13] Minutes of *Gaisgill Wesleyan Methodist Trustees Meetings*, 22.3.1900.

[14] *Ibid.*, 21.1.1930.

[15] Minutes of *Nateby Wesleyan Methodist Trustees Meetings*, 24.11.1920.

[16] Minutes of *Kirkby Stephen Wesleyan Methodist Trustees Meetings*, 20.7.1863.

[17] *Ibid.*, 3.10.1871.

[18] *Ibid.*, 1.3.1875.

[19] Minutes of the *Kirkby Stephen and Appleby Wesleyan Circuit Quarterly Meeting*, 9.6.1921; 25 were present and voting was unanimous.

[20] Minutes of the *Kirkby Stephen and Appleby Wesleyan Circuit Quarterly Meeting*, 10.12.1925.

[21] *Ibid.*, 19.9.1929.

[22] *Ibid.*, 5.6.1930.

[23] In a letter to me from *Mrs. H. Alderson, Ellerholme, Orton* (18.11.1982), great grand-daughter of John Dinsdale.

[24] Minutes of the *Kirkby Stephen and Appleby Wesleyan Circuit Quarterly Meeting*, 18.9.1930.

[25] *Ibid.*, 19.3.1931.

[26] *Ibid.*, 17.6.1931.

[27] Minutes of the *Appleby United Methodist Circuit Quarterly meeting*, 11.12.1930.

[28] Minutes of the *Brough Primitive Methodist Circuit Quarterly Meeting*, 6.9.1923.

[29] *Ibid.*, 5.6.1924.

[30] *Ibid.*, 4.12.1924.

[31] *Ibid.*, 5.3.1931.

[32] *Cumberland and Westmorland Herald*, 13.5.1972.

[33] Paul Harrington in the *Methodist Recorder*, 2.3.1978, p. 6.

[34] In a letter to me, from The Garden Flat, Morland House, Penrith, on 9.12.1982.

[35] Minutes of the *Kirkby Stephen and Appleby Wesleyan Circuit Quarterly Meeting*, 23.3.1893.

[36] *Ibid.*, 18.9.1897.

[37] Published at Kirkby Stephen.

[38] Minutes of the *Kirkby Stephen and Appleby Wesleyan Circuit Quarterly Meeting*, 12.9.1914.

[39] *Ibid.*, 12.3.1925.

[40] *Ibid.*, 13.3.1930.

[41] *Cumberland and Westmorland Advertiser*, 10.7.1860.

[42] *Ibid.*, 1.1.1861.

[43] *Ibid.*, 9.4.1861.

[44] *Ibid.*, 8.1.1867.

[45] *Ibid.*, 8.1.1867.

[46] *Mid-Cumberland and North Westmorland Herald*, 30.12.1899.

[47] *Ibid.*, 19.6.1909.

[48] *Mid-Cumberland and North Westmorland Herald*, 30.12.1899.
[49] 662, 679, 680 and 669 in the *Methodist Hymn Book*; Whittier's hymn begins "Dear Lord and Father of mankind."
[50] 676, 302, 103 and 667 in the *Methodist Hymn Book*; Whittier's hymn begins "O Lord and Master of us all."
[51] John Telford, *The Methodist Hymn-Book Illustrated* (London, 1906), p. 121, quoting Lowell.
[52] George Eskholme, *Sketch of the Life of Peter Eskholme of Summerbridge* (Bramley, 1885), p. 24.
[53] Joseph Hawkins, *O'er Hill and Dale and By the Solway Shore* (Norfolk, 1907), p. 46.
[54] George Eskholme, *Sketch of the Life of Peter Eskholme of Summer Bridge* (Bramley, 1885), p. 87.
[55] Joseph Ritson, *The Romance of Primitive Methodism* (London, 1909), p. 283.
[56] Minutes of the *Kirkby Stephen and Appleby Wesleyan Circuit Quarterly Meeting*, 23.12.1891.
[57] *Ibid.*, 19.3.1898.
[58] *Ibid.*, 14.6.1902.
[59] *Ibid.*, 20.6.1903.
[60] *Ibid.*, 19.3.1908.
[61] Minutes of the *Brough Primitive Methodist Circuit Quarterly Meeting*, 5.9.1912.
[62] Minutes of *Kirkby Stephen and Appleby Wesleyan Circuit Quarterly Meeting*, 7.6.1923.
[63] *Ibid.*, 1.3.1928.
[64] *Ibid.*, 18.12.1930.
[65] *Ibid.*, 19.3.1931.
[66] Minutes of the *Appleby United Methodist Free Church Circuit Quarterly Meeting*, 17.3.1904.
[67] *Cumberland and Westmorland Advertiser*, 25.11.1862.
[68] *Ibid.*, 9.12.1862.
[69] *Ibid.*, 6.3.1866.
[70] *Ibid.*, 9.4.1867.
[71] *Ibid.*, 3.4.1866.
[72] *Cumberland and Westmorland Herald*, 5.9.1942.
[73] *Cumberland and Westmorland Advertiser*, 27.8.1867.
[74] Minutes of the *Barnard Castle Primitive Methodist Circuit Quarterly Meeting*, March 1841.
[75] *Ibid.*
[76] *Ibid.*, March 1843.
[77] Minutes of the *Barnard Castle Primitive Methodist Local Preachers Meeting*, 23.9.1847.
[78] *Ibid.*, 23.12.1847.
[79] Minutes of the *Kirkby Stephen and Appleby Wesleyan Circuit Quarterly Meeting*, 27.9.1871.
[80] *Ibid.*, 27.9.1877.
[81] *Ibid.*, 19.12.1889.
[82] *Ibid.*, 19.9.1896.
[83] *Ibid.*, 23.6.1900.
[84] *Ibid.*, 17.3.1904.
[85] *Cumberland and Westmorland Advertiser*, 10.1.1866.
[86] *Ibid.*, 13.3.1866.
[87] John Wesley, *The Letters*, I, 173.
[88] *The Constitutional Practice and Discipline of the Methodist Church*, p. 524.
[89] John Wesley, *The Works*, VIII, 346.
[90] *Ibid.*, p. 345.
[91] *Cumberland and Westmorland Advertiser*, 20.3.1860.
[92] *Ibid.*, 10.4.1860.
[93] *Ibid.*, 29.5.1860.
[94] *Ibid.*, 19.6.1860.
[95] *Ibid.*, 25.2.1862.
[96] *Ibid.*, 13.5.1862. See also p. 16.
[97] *Ibid.*, 3.6.1862.
[98] *Ibid.*, 10.6.1862.
[99] *Ibid.*, 10.6.1862.
[100] *Ibid.*, 1.7.1862.
[101] *Ibid.*, 4.11.1862.
[102] *Ibid.*, 11.11.1862.
[103] *Ibid.*, 2.6.1863.
[104] *Ibid.*, 15.3.1864.
[105] *Ibid.*, 13.6.1865.
[106] *Ibid.*, 26.2.1867.
[107] *Ibid.*, 25.2.1868.
[108] *Ibid.*, 16.6.1868.
[109] *Ibid.*, 24.11.1868.
[110] *Ibid.*, 28.1.1879.
[111] *Ibid.*, 15.1.1889.
[112] *Ibid.*, 12.2.1889.
[113] *Ibid.*, 12.3.1889.
[114] *Ibid.*, 12.3.1889.
[115] *Ibid.*, 26.3.1889.
[116] *Ibid.*, 25.6.1889.
[117] *Mid-Cumberland and North Westmorland Herald*, 10.6.1899.

[118] *Ibid.*, 29.5.1909.
[119] *Ibid.*, 12.6.1909.
[120] *Ibid.*, 26.6.1909.
[121] *Ibid.*, 25.1.1919.
[122] *Ibid.*, 7.12.1929.
[123] *Cumberland and Westmorland Herald*, 7.5.1932.
[124] *Ibid.*, 5.9.1942.
[125] *Ibid.*, 5.7.1952.
[126] *Ibid.*, 23.6.1962.
[127] *Ibid.*, 24.6.1972.
[128] *Ibid.*, Supplement, 19.9.1981.

CHAPTER V

For a better humanity

The Methodists always made it clear that they wanted a healthier community and a better humanity and, though there were probably a few for whom social concerns appeared of greater importance than religious beliefs, they were generally consistent in worship and in missionary zeal. Yet had not other local Christian denominations the same kind of aim? And what did *they* think of the new religion which had come into the valley? Richard Burn, Vicar of Orton from 1736 to 1785, seems to have lost little sleep on account of the Wesleyan Methodists.

He dismissed these Nonconformists with brief, unruffled comments: "We have had a run of Methodism in this parish and throughout the County. By the blessed spirit of toleration and leaving them entirely to themselves, they have dwindled almost to nothing. Not having us to quarrel with, they naturally fell out amongst themselves, and are already almost all come to church again."[1] Bishop Auckland Methodists were almost in the same class. At the beginning of the eighteenth century the "then Vicar of the Parish Church informed the Bishop in answer to his Lordship's question as to whether there were any Methodists or reputed Methodists in Bishop Auckland, 'that they were of the lowest rank and few in number.' The same description might have been given of the Apostles but by these a mighty work of good was effected."[2] However fair or accurate, such comments would scarcely be made in the twentieth century as there now seems to be more brotherliness between these two branches of the Christian Church.

Baptists in the upper Eden expanded from the east, as did the Methodists. The Reverend David West, Baptist Minister at Kirkby Stephen, shows how their beginnings appear to have followed the Methodist pattern. "The Baptist work in Westmorland began in 1834 when a church was formed and a chapel built at Brough. In the years leading up to 1834, visiting preachers and evangelists had preached at Brough and made a number of converts. The leading man among these visitors was Reverend Charles Roe of Middleton-in-Teesdale . . . . Mr. Roe often came across the rough Pennine road on foot or horse to preach both at Brough and possibly other nearby villages. In 1835 the church at Brough called its first minister with financial help from Baptists in London. The work grew through the use of farmhouse preaching stations . . . at one point in the 1840's there were preaching stations at the following:- Great Asby (started in 1839). Kirkby Thore, Crosby Garrett, Whygill Head, Little Asby, Sunbiggin, Kelleth, Kirkby Stephen, Winton. The farms at Sunbiggin and Kelleth were still being used to hold services at the turn of this century . . . . The chapel at Crosby Garrett has been a Free Church place of worship since 1813 . . . . It was used by the Congregationalists at first and then shared with the Baptists and in 1856 became the sole property of the Baptists. The chapel at Great Asby was built in 1862 and the Winton chapel in 1863 . . . . The chapel building at Kirkby Stephen was opened in 1885." David West's happy conclusion is that "the relationshiop between Baptists and Methodists has grown over the years. We have alternate service times with the Methodists at Crosby Garrett and Great Asby. At Winton, Crosby Garrett and Great Asby, joint Bible Studies are held under the leadership of the Baptist Minister. These arrangements work well and overall the relationship between the two denominations is very good."[3] Methodist Local Preachers have preached in Baptist Pulpits at Great Asby, Crosby Garrett, Winton and Kirkby Stephen over the years, having first given necessary priority to the considerable preaching demands of their own scattered Circuits. On October 10th, 1982, Great Asby Baptists closed their chapel to allow the Congregation to go to Catherine Holme Methodist Harvest Festival and on November 1st, 1982, Orton Male Voice Choir (largely Methodist) sang at a Crosby Garrett Baptist Chapel Anniversary Service.[4] At the Crosby Garrett Baptist Sunday School Anniversary in June, 1892, 200 people were crammed into the Methodist Chapel.[5] The Reverend Kenneth Bounds, Superintendent of the Kirkby Stephen, Appleby and Tebay Methodist Circuit in 1980, spoke of local relationships with the Baptists. Regarding Appleby, he wrote: "Recently, the Methodist Churches, the Baptist Churches, and the Band of Hope were able to bring pressure to bear on the Town Council, and were able to change completely some of the features of a Celebration of 800 years of the granting of the Town's Borough Charter, held in the summer of 1979."[6] Baptist support must have been numerically small since their upper Eden Membership is thinly scattered. Organizationally they are probably more remote from other Baptist churches throughout the country than are the Connexional Methodists. We remember, too, that Inghamites and Methodists came to the area some 75 years before the Baptists and Methodism was fairly well established in the 1830's when Charles Roe visited Brough.

The annual Methodist Home Mission Report shows that, in the upper Eden, relationships among the Christian Churches are mainly confined to certain kinds of evangelism and occasional social witness. "There is", writes Kenneth Bounds, "a very good ecumenical spirit in the area; and we have constant fellowship with our Baptist, Anglican and Roman friends on many occasions during the year. The North Westmorland Convention which meets in Appleby in May is organized by an inter-church committee. This Convention draws about 200 or 250 people night by night for a week."[7] This state of "constant fellowship" is nevertheless confined to "occasions during the year" and does not, in any sense, belong to public Worship. The Methodist Circuit Quarterly Meetings which had to decide about organized union with the Anglicans were both solidly against the idea. There was slightly more interest in the proposed scheme in 1982 but that could be attributed to a small percentage of Methodists who had come to live in the Circuit since the earlier vote of 1972. It would now seem unlikely that Methodist and Anglican will belong to one united Church and early disappointment, shown by a few, immediately after the respective denominational votes, may well just as quickly fade away. This is the age when Methodist Ministers do not usually wear preaching gowns in the upper Eden valley and when the Local Preachers' Order of Service is, liturgically, very different from that of Anglican Worship, however much the latter may contain so-called 'modern' versions of ancient prayers or may not contain "Thou" and "Thee". In any case, there is still a measure of personal affection in the upper Eden valley when dialect speaks these ancient pronouns. Did not the Quakers do the same? Methodist Local Preachers continue to address their God, in public, in this loving and intimate manner, even though the older Church of England may now use newer forms. This is an age when, locally, particularly in small villages, the idea of a Free Church Federal Council (let alone a local Council of Churches) is quite unusual and Methodists who live in towns and cities sometimes forget how much religious isolation there can be in remote, rural areas. It may be too easy to say that such isolation is self-inflicted and that something could be done about it, but the rural scene is, for better or worse, slow to change.

Methodists, through John Wesley, do, indeed, have a historic connection with the Church of England, but they are anxious when their Anglican friends become openly enthralled with the pre-Reformation traditions and ways of the Catholic Church. Arkholme Methodist Society (in the Lancaster Methodist Circuit), as far to the south of Tebay as Spital is to the east, was an extreme example of such Methodist attitudes to other Christian denominations. During the period 1965 to 1971, the Congregation became disturbed by what they saw as dangerous trends in this ecumenical age. They refused to contribute to their Circuit Fund (part of which provides the Ministerial stipend) and spoke loud and long of the way in which Methodism was moving in the wrong direction. Among the lesser sensational paragraphs of the *Lancaster Guardian* at the time, two sentences summarised an attitude which though less vocally expressed, was to become inherently evident in the union-scheme voting of the nearby Kirkby Stephen, Appleby and Tebay Circuit: "The Arkholme Methodists . . . felt that the ecumenical movement did not represent the true gospel and true inheritance of Methodism. They were also against any relationship with the Roman Catholic Church and disapproved of Roman Catholic observers attending meetings of the Lancaster Council of Churches and being involved in council committees."[8] During this period of unrest, five young people from the Arkholme Congregation travelled to Vernoux, a small mountain village in southern France, to visit two fellow-Members of the Arkholme Society who were in charge of a Protestant

Independent Church there. These five young people belonged to Methodist farming families, near the south-Westmorland border, whose evangelical thinking had always been against the ways of the Church of England and doubly opposed to the larger Church from which the Anglicans came.

Benjamin Ingham, who, as we have seen, came briefly into the upper Eden before the Wesleyans discovered it, was himself an Anglican. Little as his influence soon proved to be, we may imagine that, locally, the Church of England believed that the instalment of evangelical preaching which was to follow him would soon, likewise, fade away. Yet Ingham's preaching tours in our area, as we have already seen, were by no means a complete failure, since they revealed his missionary concern for small, out-of-the-way places. The Inghamite Conference Minutes speak of preaching planned for Brough Sowerby, Winton, Kirkby Stephen, Crosby Garrett, Burtree, Asby, Birks, Drybeck, Brackenber, Colby, Kings Meaburn, Reagill Grange, Orton and Roundthwaite.[9] The missionary spirit was evident in remote farmhouse and hamlet and the Minutes continue:

> "On the first of June (1975) the General Overseer went to Drybeck and on that and the three following Days he visited Birks Society. He spoke with all the Members and Candidates separately and several new people. Many attended every night at the publick preaching; and on Sunday more came than Birks Chapel could contain. On Sunday morning Mr. Batty buried the first Corpse before preaching. The General Overseer catechised the Children and baptised a Child brought from over Stainmore. On Monday 5 June at the Lovefeast the General Overseer spoke of our Plan and Regulations, and received into Birks Society the following Persons, who were all present and declared their pupose to submit to Gospel Rule and Order and had Tickets given to them . . . . There is a work of Grace about Birks, which seems to be on the Increase; and it appears as if the Lord would have a Gospel Church here . . . . Several young men are effectually called, and the Souls are solid and simple. The General Overseer never received at any one time into any one Society such a number of single men so much to his satisfaction. To Thee, Lord Jesus, belongs the Glory."[10]

At a Lovefeast at Birks on June 10th, 1759, fifteen people were received as Members of the Society and twenty-eight were proposed as Candidates – all from the surrounding area.

In 1795, twenty three years after Ingham's death, his zeal was to find further and more universal expression in the founding, miles from the Eden valley, of the London Missionary Society by some Calvinistic Methodists, Independents and Scottish Presbyterians. Wesleyan Methodism, however, was neither happy with its theology nor its methods of money-raising but, equally concerned for a better humanity, it founded its own Missionary Society in 1818. This organization appionted and stationed missionaries and it was through this Conference commission that the Reverend J. Kilner was appointed as a missionary to India and Ceylon in 1848. Like other returning missionaries, he offered the challenge of his work to English Wesleyans and, recalling his visit to Penrith in April,

1865, we find his pleas for more missionaries were reported in the local Press:

"If you feel any sympathy for 200 millions of people, your fellow-subjects, subject to the same queen under British rule, given to this nation by Providence, not for scientific purpose, not for political purposes, not for commercial purposes merely, but that they may be brought to a knowledge of the truth as we possess it. Help us to bring the whole force of our national, our christianized character to bear upon them. Oh, what a noble commission! What a magnificent enterprise!"[11]

This same John Kilner was later to write to Mr. Love, in Watford: "After 17 years residence and hard work in India, I confess to feeling somewhat strange in this England of yours! I am estranged a good deal in my habits and tastes though as loyal and patriotic as ever."[12]

The importance of mission (local and worldwide) was continually kept alive and, when it was otherwise, Circuit Meetings and Itinerant Preachers brought it before the various branches of local Methodism. The Wesleyan Methodist Association Quarterly Meeting at Bolton (in 1838) agreed that " . . . a Missionary field meeting should be held on the 21 of July next to take place at half past 1 o'clock on Brakebur Hill near Bolton tool Bar in this circuit."[13] In 1851 the Associationists urged the importance of Revival, stating that they deeply deplored "the low state of piety in the Circuit and would earnestly recommend its officers and members to unit earnestly with our Minister in strenuous efforts and fervent prayer to promote a revival of the work of God. Let us consecrate ourselves afresh to the Lord, seek the entire sanctification of our hearts and by private and family prayer, attending the means of grace, inviting others to hear the gospel, and using all other consistent means labour to improve our state."[14] In a *Pastoral Address* to the Wesleyan Methodist Societies in the Appleby Circuit, in 1855, Christopher Newton and Peter Prescott encouraged mission by saying: "One thing is clear, it is high time for this Circuit to get out of its old jog-trot course: the affairs of the world move on with vigour; science is making rapid advances; and it will not do that Christians should be the only people in the world, either asleep or half-asleep . . . ."[15] The Primitive Methodist Circuit (in 1896), in thanks for mission success, recorded "with gratitude to the Great Head of the Church (its) appreciation of the self-denying and successful labours of Mr. Buck at Newbiggin during the quarter, which resulted in the conversion of over 40 souls."[16] When the Reverend John Gawthrop and the Reverend H. Waterworth came to the Kirkby Stephen Wesleyan Circuit in 1899, Joseph Lamb, the Circuit Steward, said: "The old state of grumbling and dis-content had disappeared since the old financial difficulties had gone. On the Quarterly Meeting days all was now pleasant and cheerful . . . souls had also been added to the Redeemer's Kingdom amidst the general exodus of young people to the towns which so seriously depleted their Churches."[17] Membership had increased, the second largest increase in the District. Mr. R. Iveson, Society Steward at Kirkby Stephen, said that they were to be congratulated on the fact that the Conference had not overriden their selection of Ministers. Geographically they were a large

Circuit but with two young Ministers and the Horse Hire Fund there should be no difficulty in reaching the most distant parts of the Circuit. This positive missionary outlook came in a year when local Methodism had also contributed considerable sums to the Wesleyan Century Fund. The purpose of this fund was that there should be a Methodist Chapel in every village and hamlet in the land. This Connexional idea was conceived by a layman, Mr. Perks, who believed that evangelical truths should be proclaimed everywhere.[18] By February, 1899, Crosby Garrett (with twenty poor members) had promised 27 guineas and Winton had promised or raised 43 guineas, Soulby 50 guineas, Warcop 50 guineas, Musgrave 20 guineas, and Nateby 33 guineas. Other Wesleyan Societies had yet to declare their targets but 1000 guineas looked like being the Circuit total. Locally and nationally, Wesleyan Methodism was showing new missionary concern, and, within our area, new territorial boundaries would need fixing and keeping, while constant 'missioning' and re-missioning' took place.

Each Society, as we have already seen, maintained an overseas missionary interest. The Leaders' Meeting appointed its local Missionary Collector and, for example, Mrs. E. A. Clarke, of Kirkby Thore, kept in regular touch with most of the membership of the Society between 1962 and 1966. Annually, she collected sums ranging from £2.2.6 to £2.8.0, such subscriptions coming from some twenty people. Other accredited Collectors in the other Societies also carried their *Adult Collector's Book,* on the back of which was printed "The Methodist Missionary Society . . . has Missions in Ceylon, India, Burma, South-East Asia, Rhodesia, West Africa, Kenya, West Indies, Central and South America. As auxiliaries of incessant Evangelisation it has Colleges, Day Schools, Sunday Schools, Hospitals, Dispensaries, Leper Asylums, Orphanages, Industrial Schools, Refuges, etc., etc." Added to these annual sums was the Offertory from one Sunday's Collection and from that taken at the annual Missionary evening. In 1927, the Wesleyan Circuit total thus amounted to £270.7.7.[19] The Circuit Missionary total for 1980 was approximately £772.57,[20] though in addition, some £300 was collected by children and young people for Junior Missionary Association funds. While the 1927 Wesleyan total would, as we have said, have almost paid for another Minister in the local Circuit, the 1980 total would, however, be somewhat short of approximately £4,200 required as the stipend for a 1980 Methodist Minister.

Eden Methodist congregations clearly believed that their goal of expansion, either in the local area or thousands of miles away, would also make for a better humanity: a humanity, that is, which must know about Christ and make the required response. If the Church of England had similar concern, its ways of showing it were quite different: so much so, that the two Denominations did not often work or worship together. They did, however, fight together: in wars that were also supposed to cleanse humanity. For, as with the Established Church, the Methodists were never forbidden, by their Conferences, to take up arms.

The earlier Quaker influence had not been passed down to Methodists of later generations, and because exemptions from military service were granted to those required for agricultural work in the 1939-1945 War, the principles of individual Conscientious Objectors were not often brought to the test. Thus a Methodist Conscientious Objector living near Appleby, in 1940, was one of a very few (perhaps the only one) from our holy community. He had to meet a Tribunal of four people at Carlisle and state his convictions about taking up arms against an enemy. The Methodist Minister at Appleby, the Reverend Clifford Brown, had been a Pacifist in the 1914-1918 War and had suffered imprisonment at Dartmoor for his views. He was, therefore, a strong support for the young farmworker who, with the added advocacy of Joseph C. Salkeld (a teacher and Methodist Preacher who had served in the First World War), was granted exemption from military service - provided he stayed in agricultural employment. Here was a young man who did not have the support which Methodist Conferences had given more whole heartedly in other matters of Christian Citizenship. Yet he reached this difficult decision almost entirely on his own, unshaken in his convictions.

There had been, however, no Methodist tradition of Pacifism, John Wesley himself not being entirely clear about where he stood. In his lengthy and amazing dissertation entitled *The Doctrine of Original Sin* he saw armed aggression in all its horror. He could not imagine that even "a Heathen" would allow any place in society for wars. Some soldiers, he thought, were lacking in honour: ". . . Catholic soldiers . . . who broke into the house of a poor countryman in Flanders, butchered him and his wife, with five or six children; and after they had finished their work, sat down to enjoy the fruit of their labour. But in the midst of their meal conscience awaked. One of them started up in great emotion, and cried out, 'O Lord! what have I done? As I hope for salvation, I have eaten flesh in Lent!' "[21] He followed these scathing remarks with further blasts: "It was conscience, no question, which induced so many of the Dukes of Savoy, notwithstanding the public faith engaged over and over, to shed the blood of their loyal subjects, the Vaudois, like water, to ravage their fields, and destroy their cities. What but conscience could move the good Catholics of a neighbouring kingdom, in the last century, to murder (according to their own account) two hundred and fifteen thousand Protestants in six months?"[22] For surely, he says, "all our declamations on the strength of human reason, and the eminence of our virtues, are no more than the cant and jargon of pride and ignorance, so long as there is such a thing as war in the world. Men in general can never be allowed to be reasonable creatures, till they know not war any more. So long as this monster stalks uncontrolled, where is reason, virtue, humanity?"[23] Yet earlier in the year in which he made these attacks (1756), he was himself ready to gather an army of at least 200 volunteers to be placed at the King's pleasure![24] By 1779 he seemed to be seeing preparations for war in an entirely new light: "The alarm has been general in England as well as Ireland, particularly in the maritime parts. But it has done abundantly more good than harm to the work of God. The children of God have been greatly stirred up and have been more (instant) in prayer. And many men of the world have been greatly awakened, and continue so to this day. Most of those who have the fullest intercourse with God believe our enemies will never be permitted to land in England. And, indeed, God has already given abundant proof of His hearing prayer: first, in their not landing at Plymouth, where they stayed gaping and staring for eight-and-forty hours while they might with all ease have destroyed both the dock and the town; secondly, in the malignant fever which has broken out in their fleet, and already destroyed several thousands of men."[25]

After Wesley's day, the various branches of Methodism were not able to advise strongly against taking up of arms. Instead, they were ready to supply Chaplains if Circuits were adequately staffed. There was no shortage of volunteers. "The Rev. E. Ogden announced that he had offered himself for service in the war, and wished to know if the circuit would release him for such duties."[26] The Circuit, however, did not think it could manage without him. In May 1982, the Reverend John K. Watson, R.N., went as Methodist Chaplain with the South Atlantic Task Force and later wrote, in the annual Home Mission Report (1983): "I would have preferred diplomacy and reason to have succeeded but it did not and grim though the lesson may be, aggression can often only be countered by the disciplined application of force."[27]

The 1914-1918 War was a disaster for Methodism. The Wesleyan Connexion produced a report in 1918 which spoke of large numbers of deaths of soldier-Local Preachers and regretted that they included a high proportion of the most vigorous and effective preachers. Those returning would need a hearty welcome back. "Give them an opportunity to tell you their experience; encourage them, and make it easy for them to carry their message of the sustaining grace of God in presence of hardship, danger and death to the congregations in your Circuit."[28] The Second Brough Primitive Methodist Baptismal Register (17.9.1885-30.4.1933) contains the names of young fathers who were serving in the Kings Royal Rifles (1915), the 22nd Regiment Durham Light Infantry (1916), the 3rd Border Regiment Light Infantry (1916), the King's Own Yorkshire Light Infantry (1917) and the 4th West Yorkshire Light Infantry (1917). Brough Primitive Methodist Local Preachers were informed in December, 1915, that "Bro. Herbert S. Lawson (had) left College to serve in the R.A.M.C." and that "Brother James Brown, assistant Society Steward, Kirkby Stepehn, and local preacher, (had) left to serve in the A.S.C."[29] In January 1919, the local *Herald* reported that Reverend Ernest Ogden, the Kirkby Stephen Wesleyan Minister, had conducted a memorial Service for those from the

Circuit who had fallen in the War. The young Methodist population of this remote area had been sadly reduced.

We should remember, however, that the three branches of Methodism in the upper Eden valley did, occasionally, express their views about war and peace. In March 1911, the Wesleyan "Revd. R. E. Little submitted a memorial for the Treaty of Peace which was received with much approval and passed and it was decided that Copies be sent to the Prime Minister, The Speaker and the various Members of Parliament who represent the Circuit."[30] The Brough Primitives agreed (in March, 1921) "to bring before our people the claims of the League of Nations, and urge our people to join the local branch at Kirkby Stepehn."[31] The Wesleyan Circuit unanimously agreed (in September, 1922) to urge "the Government to use every endeavour to settle the dispute with Turkey without recourse to war; and that copies of this resolution be forwarded to the Prime Minister and the Member for the County."[32] In December 1927, Wesleyans sent greetings to the League of Nations, saying they desired "to express . . . high appreciation of every effort calculated to promote peace on earth and goodwill to men. (They) also pledge. . . to continue to pray that the League may ever be guided by tthe Spirit of the Most High, believing . . . that it is righteousness alone that exalteth a nation, and that the supreme end of life is to seek first the Kingdom of God and His Righteousness."[33] In June 1928, they expressed great joy that the Government was seriously discussing "the most important question of the Outlawry of War."[34] In December 1931, the Brough Primitive Circuit agreed that "January 3rd be a day of Prayer for the World Disarmament."[35] In June 1932, at the United Methodist Circuit Quarterly Meeting, a "letter was read on the Armament Question and we were resolved to do all in our power for the total abolition of war."[36]

In spite of these aspirations, the earlier Quaker tradition of non-violence was not to find expression in the beliefs and practices of the Methodists. Was it, then, divine retribution that thus, numerically, the strength of Methodism was so considerably reduced? Did Methodist participation in war negate the high principle of a better humanity for all the world? Or did it help to protect the freedom to believe in that Deity who, for nearly two hundred years, had transformed the religious life of the upper Eden? Though none of us can say, we nevertheless wonder what might yet be the potential - or the predicament - of this holy community.

---

[1] From a letter of Richard Burn to Charles Lyttleton, Bishop of Carlisle, of 2.8.1763, contained in the Stowe Manuscript 754, folio 112. (In the British Library).

[2] Matthew Braithwaite, *History of Wesleyan Methodism in the Bishop Auckland Circuit* (Bishop Auckland, 1885), p. 31.

[3] In a letter to me, from 70 South Road, Kirkby Stephen, on 23.11.1982.

[4] Duplicated Plan (October 3rd, 1982 to January 2nd, 1983) of the Westmorland Group of Baptist Churches.

[5] The Reverend Bernard E. Umpleby, *Crosby Garrett Methodist Chapel 1882-1982* (Centenary Celebrations Leaflet, 1982). Berned E. Umpleby is a Minister in the Kirkby Stephen section of the circuit.

[6] The Reverend Kenneth Bounds, "From Lakes To Pennine Way" in *Down To Earth* (The Methodist Home Mission Report, Westminster, 1980), p. 43.

[7] *Ibid.*, p. 43.

[8] *Lancaster Guardian*, 7.5.1971.

[9] *Minutes of the Inghamites*, 1755-1760. The Plan was fixed at Wheatley, near Burnley. The time was Easter, 1758, and the arrangements were for the quarter April-June, 1758.

[10] *Ibid.*, recording the impact of Ingham's preaching; Ingham is known as the 'General Overseer'.

[11] *Cumberland and Westmorland Advertiser*, 2.5.1865.

[12] In a letter deated 19.5.1865, addressed to 9 Carey Place, Watford.

[13] Minutes of the *Appleby Wesleyan Methodist Association Circuit Quarterly Meeting*, 27.6.1838.

[14] *Ibid.*, 22.9.1851.

[15] Delivered to a meeting of a special Circuit Committee held at Appleby on 17.2.1855. This *Pastoral Address* was presented by the two Travelling Preachers here named.

[16] Minutes of the *Brough Primitive Methodist Circuit Quaterly Meeting*, 5.3.1896.

[17] *Mid-Cumberland and North Westmorland Herald*, 9.9.1899.

[18] *Ibid.*, 14.1.1899.

[19] See page 80 for other Circuit totals during the 1920's.

[20] In four of the 36 Societies no figures were available, but in consultation with Mrs. M. M. Ewin, Hollow Green, Raisbeck, the Circuit Overseas Treasurer, we included their 1979 contributions for the purpose of reaching a total.

[21] John Wesley, *The Works*, IX, 218.

[22] *Ibid.*, p. 218.

[23] *Ibid.*, p. 223.

[24] John Wesley, *The Letters*, III, 165.

[25] *Ibid.*, VI, 358.

[26] Minutes of the *Kirkby Stephen, Appleby and Sedbergh Wesleyan Circuit Quarterly Meeting*, 13.6.1918.

[27] Reverend John K. Watson, "5 Days in May", in *Body and Soul* (Report of the Methodist Church Home Mission Division, London, 1983), p. 12.

[28] Report of the *Wesleyan Connexional Local Preachers Committee* to the Manchester Conference, 1918.

[29] Minutes of the *Brough Primitive Methodist Circuit and Local Preachers Meeting*, 2.12.1915.

[30] Minutes of the *Kirkby Stephen and Appleby Wesleyan Circuit Quarterly Meeting*, 23.3.1911.

[31] Minutes of the *Brough Primitive Methodist Circuit Quarterly Meeting*, 4.3.1921.

[32] Minutes of the *Kirkby Stephen and Appleby Wesleyan Circuit Quarterly Meeting*, 21.9.1922.

[33] *Ibid.*, 8.12.1927.

[34] *Ibid.*, 14.6.1928.

[35] Minutes of the *Brough Primitive Methodist Circuit Quarterly Meeting*, 3.12.1931.

[36] Minutes of the *Appleby United Methodist Circuit Quarterly Meeting*, 9.6.1932.

CHAPTER VI
"The life of God in the soul of man"
(John Wesley)

We are able to speak of the Eden Methodists as a holy community if we remember that John Wesley's definition of holiness was:"The life of God in the soul of man"; and when we understand the beliefs and practices of holy communities, we are part-way towards seeing their potential as living religion which must grow rather than fade away. Nevertheless, as Pamela Luke said (in 1982), as Vice President of the Methodist Conference:

"It is difficult for anyone who has neither been a member of a small church, nor known one intimately, to understand the feelings of those who do belong, who are loyal, who have a deep ccommitment to Christ, a sense of mission and, who over many years, have received little encouragement either by increase in numbers or by the recognition of their position by the Church as a whole".[1]

In our last chapter, therefore, we look a little more closely at these holy people and their ways, concerned that fellow-Methodists, in town and city, do not forget this (or any other) rural Methodism. For while men of missionary zeal have left this second Eden to share their faith with people far away, others have remained behind and have put all their energy into the work already begun: a work which still goes on, static on some frontiers but dynamic on others. Robert Hutchinson, for example, who went as a missionary to China from Winton, at the beginning of this century, was to write back to Mr. Barker, from the Wesleyan Mission at Canton:

"It is good of an evening to have a little walk out in the grounds by oneself, with the stars shining so peacefully overhead, and to think of the old times at Winton, to hum the hymns we used to sing, to call to mind the experiences given in the class meetings, and to fight over again the battles of winter prayer meetings, when souls had to be grappled for and pulled into the Kingdom."[2]

God will not - and we should not - forget either Hutchinson's zeal or Winton's prayers.

The Chapel of the upper Eden is much the same size as the home from which its people come and it is furnished with the same functional simplicity. Members of the small Congregation, like the family at home, need a minimum of symbolism to bind them together and, for example, if a Cross is to be seen (though generally it is not), one feels that it will be a *small* Cross. The Bread and Wine of the Lord's Supper (taking place about once every three months) symbolize the Body and Blood of Jesus but not with Catholic intensity. They are the symbols of the continuing and sacrifical love of Our Lord. The Baptismal font is often very small and unobtrusively placed; were it bigger it might be safely placed near the door, a symbol, indeed, of early entry into the Congregation of Christ's flock. The Chapels themselves are sometimes referred to as "Houses of Prayer" and, in this sense, visual aids are superfluous. A Congregation 'at prayer' relies on faith rather than sight. It is the Pulpit which is usually central and obvious, signifying the importance of Preaching from the Holy Scriptures. The Chapel windows are usually without much colour, large enough to bring in the light of day or to shine out into the world's darkness during evening Worship. Many of these Chapels are almost isolated from that world of symbolism and of colour which belongs to hundreds of millions of people who believe themselves to be worshipping the same God.

Since, then, symbols appear to have a secondary importance in the worship of our holy people, what sacred actions take place which both bind the Congregations together and say something about the God who is worshipped? We must remember that the atmosphere of worship is one of quietness. The created world outside is also quiet, though this is more true of the weekday working environment than of the Sunday 'worldly' noises which increasingly disturb the Sabbath rest. The Sabbath, as with the Jews, is not for action; action takes place the day before. As Moses had said: "Tomorrow is a day of solemn rest, a holy Sabbath to the Lord";[3] and it would seem that sacred acts, or action, in the Chapels, are as few and as quiet as possible, except those involved in singing and preaching. No bell calls the Congregation to worship and no bell will ring when the Bread is consecrated. Few responsive "Amens" will be heard and even the Lord's Prayer may be uttered by the Preacher alone. The atmosphere is repeating the creativity of God. Nature's creative power is rarely noisy, seeds waiting quietly in the soil in the winter and ripening under a silent, summer sun. Nothing should be *done* in worship, least it suggests that God has not done enough. In His good time, He has created and He has redeemed and man may not hurry Him. Rufus Jones might almost have called our Methodists "mystical",[4] like the Seekers, for they have demonstrated "a genuine spiritual quest for something deeper than the empty show of religion, a search for what some of them happily call 'an upper room Christianity' . . . They knew little of the history of the spiritual travail of the race, and they evidently undervalued external helps . . . But they preferred to wait for God Himself to show his face rather than to bow down before the images which men had set up for them to worship".

As far, then, as sacred acts are concerned, the Preacher is the busiest sacred person, and so it is thus an extreme disappointment when he does not keep his Pulpit engagement. For it is the Preacher who says the public, informal prayers and who reads and interprets the Bible to his Congregation. It is the Preacher who invites the Congregation to make an offering; this is always monetary, though occasionally he also asks for the offering or dedicated commitment of the whole of the worshippers' lives. When an Offertory is brought to the "altar" (barely discernible in the Chapels) by one unaccustomed to doing so, he sometimes does not quite know where it should be placed, since the Holy Communion Table, though sacred, is not more so than the rest of the Chapel. In this, we are reminded, as Kristensen points out, of the Great Round Altar, near Peking (China), where temple and altar seem to have become almost one, and the same.[5] The aisle of the Eden Chapel is as sacred as the area to which it leads.

Holy Baptism is a sacred act more rare than the Sacrament of the Lord's Supper. Generally administered to infants, it may also be conducted for older people. The use of water in this religious act, as in so many religions, relates to rebirth. The Methodist prayer is that the child will experience a new life in Christ and then formally and publicly join His Church. Those parents not fully committed to the life and worship of the local Methodist community, knowing, nevertheless, that such baptism is "in the name of Jesus", may be bringing their child in the hope of protecting it from illness or danger, but this is less than the full meaning of the Sacrament.

Unlike the Jews whose "holy days" are linked with the destinies and ideals of the Jewish people, Christians have prepared their sacred calendars around the life of Jesus. Eden Methodists, unlike some Christians, have excluded the Saints Days though they have other annual celebrations which recall what God has done and is doing for His world. And just as space, as we shall see, is set aside for the possibility of a person or persons being where God may appear again, so it is with sacred time. Persons will return to a place, at a particular time, perhaps at a Sunday School Anniversary, hoping, at best, that their god will do for them what he did the previous year, or, at least, will somehow act again for them. In addition to the weekly Services (commemorating creation and redemption), there are particular Services when God's goodness is recalled and related, as in the annual Covenant Service early in the New Year. There is also the Harvest Festival when, again, God's providence is re-presented, and there are two other Anniversaries which are sacred times, though these may well seem to reflect what man has often done for God rather than what God has once done for man; they are the Sunday School and Chapel Anniversaries.

The Covenant Service became increasingly dear to John Wesley and it is still shared in the upper Eden valley, year by year. On Christmas Day, 1747, he wrote in his Journal: "Both this and the following days I strongly urged the wholly giving up ourselves to God, and renewing in every point our covenant that the Lord should be our God."[6] On August 6th, 1755, he wrote again of the blessing of joining in a covenant to serve God, and at Spitalfields, on August 11th, 1755, "all the people stood up, in testimony of assent, to the number of about eighteen hundred persons. Such a night I scarce ever saw before. Surely the fruit of it shall remain forever."[7] By 1770, his Covenant Services were beginning to take place at the very beginning of the year and on December 31st, 1771, he conducted a Watch-night Service to usher in the New Year with singing and prayer before his usual Covenant Service the following day at Spitalfields.[8] By 1775, again in London, on January 1st, an excessive congregation shared in this annual service and "Afterwards many desired to return thanks, either for a sense of pardon, for full salvation, or for a fresh manifestation of His grave, healing all their backslidings."[9] At his Covenant Service on January 1st, 1777, "many found his power present to heal, and were enabled to urge their way with strength renewed."[10] On January 1st, 1782, at covenant renewal, "the dread of God, in an eminent degree, fell upon the whole congregation."[11] Each succeeding Covenant Service seemed better than the last. At that rate, they should surely now be the highlight of the Methodist year, but this is not, alas, obviously so. Fine as the Order of Service had been for many years, numbers attending are rarely excessive; it contains, of course, already-prepared prayers. Even so, it continues, and there seems something wrong with a year which does not begin with it. Its purpose is still that of renewal of dedication to an unfailing God and its timing is tied to the turn of the year when, as Charles Wesley says:

"Our life is a dream
Our time as a stream
Glides swiftly away,
And the fugitive moment refuses to stay."[12]

The Harvest Festival also celebrates the goodness of God but the note of dedicated renewal is by no means so strong. The symbols of God's goodness and creation are displayed on every available ledge in the Chapel, yet the Covenant Service, held at a time when there may not even be a symbolic vase of flowers, has far more personal challenge in its prayers and vows. Though the Harvest Festival may be described as a "sacred time", the Services (as we have already seen) were sources of income rather than times of renewed dedication in response to God's continuing bounty. As for the annual Sunday School Anniversary, as we have also seen, it tends to reflect past efforts of teachers and scholars rather than encourage re-dedication of parents. As with the Chapel Anniversary, the Congregation is probably seeing what Methodism has done, in the past year, with what God has given; it is the year that has gone, rather than what the re-creating God can do in the year that is to come, which seems more important.

It is, of course, in the Chapel that the awareness of the presence of God is best experienced. Among the Canaanites, divine theophanies were at high places such as Horeb and Sinai but the Deuteronomic Reformation of the seventh century (BC) centralised all worship in Jerusalem. So in Deuteronomy 12, verse 2, we read: "You shall surely destroy all the places where the nations whom you shall disposses served their gods, upon the high mountains and upon the hills and under every green tree." To Zion, the holy hill of Jerusalem, the Jews would be drawn to celebrate their deliverance. To Zion, Jesus and his parents "went up according to custom" (Luke 2, verse 42), and to Zion, Methodists also climb. In spite of the fact that Winton Chapel is on level ground, Robert Hutchinson's missionary letter from China (in 1906) begins by saying: "I make mention of you all at the Father's Throne, and also the little hill of Zion established at Winton."[13]

The hymn book, from which Winton and other Methodists sing, has a small section of 26 hymns entitled *Worship in the Sanctuary* in which the Chapel is seen as a place where inner conflicts and sins may be exposed to God: the concept of height (God above) being complemented by that of depth (man below). Henry M. Butler, for example, writes thus:

"Lift every gift that Thou Thyself has given;
Low lies the best till lifted up to heaven:
Low lie the bounding heart, the teeming brain,
Till, sent from God, they mount to God again."[14]

Uniting the two is man's readiness to offer the whole of life as a sacrifice, described by Charles Wesley in a hymn of dedication:

"O Thou who camest from above,
The pure celestial fire to impart,
Kindle a flame of sacred love
On the mean altar of my heart!"[15]

But it is the God above who ignites the spark and only death which makes "the sacrifice complete."[16] Isaac Watts, in showing how the sacred space is both God's house and house of prayer (reflecting the feelings of the Psalmist),[17] suggests that the way in which man finally discovers how to share God's heavenly happiness is by keeping unceasing company with Him on earth:

"Lord of the worlds above,
How pleasant and how fair
The dwellings of Thy love,
Thine earthly temples are!
To Thine abode
My heart aspires,
With warm desires
To see my God.
"O happy souls that pray
Where God delights to hear!
O happy men that pay
Their constant service there!
They praise Thee still,
And happy they
Who love the way
To Zion's hill!"[18]

When first Methodist Preachers came to the upper Eden valley, it was to preach in the open-air or in a house. As time went by, the house became too small and alternative sacred space was required. Who, then, could enter it? Only those who had been fully persuaded by the message of the Preachers? Those who wanted to hear the message again before making a response? Or those who might hear it for the very first time? How, in fact, did one become a Member of the Methodist Church? As Robert Hutchinson discovered, the requirements in China were somewhat different from those in England: "In Methodism at home one hears next to nothing of knowledge, knowledge of our doctrines and of the way of salvation, but out here everything seems to turn on it. If a man wants to become a Christian he goes to our Catechist, who straightaway teaches him the doctrine for six months or so, during which time the man ceases to worship idols, throws overboard his extra wives and conforms to our rules, then he is baptised and becomes a Member of the Church."[19] With no extra wives and no apparent idols, entry into the Eden Methodist Community has been somewhat less mechanical and, in any case, the Chapel doors have always been open even for "strangers", (as a few persistently, but unlovingly call them).

Generally speaking, initiation (that is, the later post-Baptismal initiation) into the upper Eden Methodist community has been both informal and formal, but always in public. The first has been by conversion, the second by 'Reception into Membership.' Sometimes there may have been one without the other. Sometimes the second has followed the first, sometimes it has preceded it. Conversion has been the public response to preaching: an admission by the convert that he has found deliverance from his sins. But sometimes this experience has followed the Service in which Membership has been officially recognized and that has not been inappropriate, since he who became a Member was actually desiring to be saved from his sins. Some who were converted never joined the Methodist Society, although they were always welcomed at the Chapel. Such adherents, however, were not able to hold important office in the local Methodist Society. As in wider Methodism, those who became Members received a quarterly (now often yearly) Membership ticket, a valued token: "Some members treasured their tickets as signs of unbroken precious fellowship until the close of life: and dying, asked that they might be interred with them."[20] This was not so much a way of arranging "provisions" to accompany them in their new life but an expression of their entire confidence that Jesus has been their personal Saviour and Friend: One who had always loved them and who would continue to do so.

The privilege of becoming a Member of the Methodist Church in a particular, local Society is now no less glorious, as the recognized basic requirements show: "All those who confess Jesus Christ as Lord and Saviour and accept the obligation to serve Him in the life of the Church and the world are welcome as full members of the Methodist Church."[21] Conversion is implied, the new life requiring dedicated service. The Sacrament of Infant Baptism has introduced the child into the sacred community and the intended outcome is discipleship in the Membership of the Church. As we have seen, attendance at the Sunday School has not always led to Membership of the Church, though it is still seen as one way of giving that Christian instruction which is a vital part of preparation. The requirement of the Methodist Church says (but here there is no reference to the traditional Sunday School) that " . . . classes shall be generally established which shall directly provide for the religious instruction of young people. The object of these classes shall be to secure the decision of children for Christ their instruction and training in Christian Doctrine and ethics and the development in Christian experience and character. The Holy Scripture shall be the basis of instruction and these classes shall be met wherever possible weekly."[22] The moment of decision concerning actual Membership comes after a short course of teaching and challenge, in which privileges and duties are outlined: "It is", says the Methodist requirement, "the privilege and duty of Members of the Methodist Church to avail themselves of the two sacraments namely Baptism and the Lord's Supper. As membership of The Methodist Church also involves fellowship it is the duty of all Members of the Methodist Church to seek to cultivate this in every possible way."[23]

All, then, who wish to enter sacred space may do so. They thus become sacred persons, for there they hear the way in which they should live and die – the way in which they will receive divine approval or disapproval. They are in the presence of the sacred, or the holy, and whatever response they make, it must take account of the fact that they have been in the environment of the deity, in sacred space, in sacred time and among His holy people. Thenceforth they must be consecrated to one god or another. To this extent they have become sacred, like Uzzah. Oxen, carrying the Ark of the Lord on a new cart, stumbled and Uzzah steadied the Ark, but the Lord was angry because he touched the Ark and Uzzah dropped down dead.[24] He had involved himself with a sacred object and therefore he had to behave accordingly. Inviting someone to go inside an Eden Chapel is a serious matter!

The Methodist Deity is God the Father, God the Son and God the Holy Spirit, three Persons in one God, to whom the most-often repeated prayer is "Our Father who art in heaven", as Jesus required.[25] The Deity of the Eden Methodists is altogether revealed in Jesus, Son of the Father "who art in heaven."

God the Holy spirit is the God who reassures the convert that he is in a new and intimate relationship with God the Father[26] and who enables him to practise love, joy, peace, patience, kindness, goodness, faithfulness, gentleness and self-control:[27] those virtues which combined in the life of God the Son. One senses, therefore, the frustration (if not sheer amazement) as Robert Hutchinson begins his missionary labours in China, where ancient religion had worshipped sky, earth, clouds, winds, mountains, rivers and seas. Better acquainted with the words of Winton than with the colloquialisms of Canton, his early observations solemnly reflected the size of the task before him:

> As we come up and down the rivers there are scores of temples on the banks . . . There is the earth demon who would get out and ruin everything if they made holes in the earth, so that they are extremely loathe to do any mining, though there is enough mineral wealth to make them a rich nation . . . There is a river dragon, so that it is very difficult to get a Chinaman to get into the water . . ."[28]

Dialogue between different religions would have been useful, even in China in 1906. Here, in the Eden of 1981, it was far from being a popular idea.

On August 29th, H. C. Little wrote:

"You report that a Persian lady is in the Penrith district to spread the Bahai faith . . . Although the tenets of this faith might appear to be promising, they are no better than some of the other fringe religions that seem to have taken seed in Britain."

On September 5th, Miss F. Kamtarin wrote:

"I would say that it is neither a fringe religion nor a sect. It is an independent world-wide religion which has its own profound and beautiful scriptures. If the followers of Jesus had remained in the Holy Land, Christianity would not have spread to Europe. It did not matter then and it does not matter now, which race or nationality spread the message of God . . . Baha'is believe in the oneness of mankind, the fundamental oneness of religion . . . As one comes to appreciate the significance of this revelation it obviously becomes an honour to share this gift with all people."

On September 12th, an Adrian Little, of Lazonby, near Penrith, then replied:

"As a Christian who has read little of the Baha'is writings and spoken to no-one who practises its teachings . . ."[29]

and proceeded, paragraph by paragraph, to close the door on much further discussion. Little by Little the dialogue came to an end.

Our two prints of Circuit Plans[30] point to the importance of sacred word to the sacred community of the upper Eden. The frequent public interpretation of the Holy Bible by the Preacher, however, was not based upon what he himself thought about its message, but upon what God was compelling him to say through its sacred verses. The Scriptures, themselves, thus had a unique authority and even the printed edges of the old Plans had a particular style because they were the precious documents which announced the coming of God's chosen messengers. A Scripture text was often printed on the Plan, an aid to the devotional preparation necessary before Sunday Worship. On current, functional Plans, both decoration and texts are missing, lost in the modern age.

One recalls, from sermons between 1944 and 1952, at Catherine Holme Methodist Chapel, that there was an emphasis on Old Testament preaching, especially from the eschatological content of the prophets Amos, Jeremiah, Isaiah and Exekiel. Like the Old Testament characters who apparently inspired the Eden preaching, it seemed that the mid-twentieth-century preachers were sincerely and passionately convinced as they brought their urgent messages of imminent doom. But one is doubtful whether these preachers shared the Old Testament prophets' interest in politics. Doubtful, too, whether recollections of adolescence are sufficiently objective to be historically accurate, three Circuit Methodists were invited to monitor sermon themes during ten weeks from December, 1982, to February, 1983. Hettie Alderson (At Orton), Trevor Capstick (at Kirkby

Stephen) and Stephen Dent (at Bolton) were all able to report that preaching was no longer largely confined to the Old Testament, nor was it especially eschatalogical – even though some of their observations had taken place during Advent.

Local Preachers of the early 1980's were also invited to comment on their preaching experience: their sharing of the sacred word. John Thornborrow, a Local Preacher from Tebay, who had been preaching for 55 years, said how members of the Congregations had sometimes said to him that "because they had heard the Word of God preached simply but sincerely, God had become more real to them." He recalled how he once "felt led to make an appeal in a few simple words, in the old-fashioned way. A young man came forward form the back of the Chapel and kneeling at the Communion rail, made a decision to given his life to Christ." He spoke, too, of someone who had been enabled to rise above her despairing condition with a "new hope and a new experience of God."[31] Harold Alderson, a Local Preacher from Orton, who became an accredited Preacher in 1946 (while farming at Catherine Holme), said that he had preached "Jesus and Him crucified, raised from the dead and alive in our midst in this present day. It is then", he continued, "that people become aware of God's power and His presence and have a desire to seek His presence for themselves." Hearers make a response to this awareness by discovering "their own personal need of a Saviour . . . their need to repent of their sins and be forgiven." He recalled how a particular hearer, guided by the Holy Spirit, experienced forgiveness and was miraculously made whole.[32]

Both John Thornborrow and Harold Alderson have proclaimed the sacred word among their own people and the two hearers who made visible response to their preaching both became actively involved in their local Methodist Community. The two Preachers believed themselves to be called, years ago, by God, to deliver the sacred word and their lifelong compulsion rests on the authority of that sacred word. Trevor Capstick, then a young Local Preacher at Kirkby Stephen, following in the same succession, said: "I try to ensure my preaching is BIBLE-BASED, trying to allow the Bible to speak for itself, for it is God's Word to men."[33] One result of this kind of Eden Methodist preaching was that, as local obituaries point out, people died in faith and hope. William Brogden, for example, Primitive Methodist in the Brough Branch of the Barnard Castle Circuit, died on March 27th, 1847 (at the age of 75). "During his last illness his confidence in God was unshaken and his peace and joy were unspeakable. He would often say 'I am going home'."[34] William Moister, Travelling Preacher, born at Sedbergh in 1808, died in 1891. His obituary says, interestingly, that on Sunday, August the ninth, 1891, "He peacefully entered into life."[35]

Bible-based preaching could, however, easily point to a wicked world since, as the New Testament shows, the world is the arena of temptation, and friendship with it is "emnity with God."[36] It is full of the immoral, the greedy, robbers and idolators, though, as Paul points out, to avoid such altogether, one would have to leave the world completely.[37] James says that what really matters is that a follower of Jesus should keep himself unstained from the world,[38] a world which, as John says, though it was made through Him,[34] hates Jesus because He testifies of it that "its works are evil".[40] So our local Methodist emphases have shown that society is regarded as much a power for evil as for good and that is worldly pleasures can spoil lives and separate men from God. The Baptismal Prayer, offered towards the end of the Sacrament, said: "Grant that (he) may have power and strength to have victory, and to triumph over the world, the flesh and the devil."[41] Even so, as we have seen, many Methodist males marched with non-Methodists, right into 'worldly' wars and fought side-by-side with some, at least, who may even have been unbelievers.

'Mixing' with 'the world' was, therefore, always a sensitive area of choice and decision. Choosing a leader to replace one whose interest had lapsed or who had died, or who had emigrated, became an unenviable task if there were few to choose from. In the search for one who had comparable gifts and ability, moral and religious standards (above those of 'the world') had to be upheld. Yet, miraculously, over two and a quarter centuries, lay leadership, which has always been of significant importance for Methodism, has been faithfully maintained and men and women have been appointed to office without any compromise in standards. So also have preachers been found to ensure that at least one Service took place each Sunday at every Methodist Society throughout the Circuit. Even the society of the surrounding villages seemed to want a man of integrity at the Chapel, someone who was "above the ordinary", a saint among weaker varieties.

Pamela Luke also said to the Methodist Conference (in 1982):

> "It is difficult to attract new members to a small number where any particular age group may be represented by only one or two people and where the majority are likely to be among the elderly. Any sense of mission and outreach is extinct or lies dormant, waiting for an injection of hope to bring it to life again with the conviction that renewal is possible."[42]

We do not, therefore, forget Mr. and Mrs. Brunskill and their family: they were at the very beginning of our upper Eden Methodism. For years they were small in number, possibly none too young. But is is unlikely that they simply looked out over Stainmore's "wintry waste" and wondered why the Revival was so long reaching them, especially since renewal was never more necessary that when the Inghamite movement crumbled and the Methodist advance tarried. What they had to do was to make clear, as best they could (to the few that were there to listen), that Ingham's enchanting preaching, though not entirely doctrinally acceptable, had contained elements which should be treasured and made more widely known: embers which should be fanned into a new flame.

The waters of the Eden come from above and they also spring from the earth itself, some from what can only be called "stony ground". Drybeck, an

Eden tributary, almost disappears in a dry summer but thirsty livestock know the wherabouts of a spring which rises just at the edge of the river-bed and which renews their lives just when resources from elsewhere seem to have failed. Renewal, when all else seems to have failed, can come out of an apparently dying movement. Anna L. Waring may have made this important discovery when she wrote, in Victorian style;

"I thirst for springs of heavenly life,
And here all day they rise;
I seek the treasure of Thy Love,
And close at hand it lies".[43]

Bede Griffiths, in his book "Return To The Centre" (1978) also appreciated this but did not take it for granted that everyone would know how to reach the spring. He stressed that for religion to be renewed from within, it would have to find new ways of telling people what it believed, new ways of clarifying its ritual and new ways of organizing itself so that the original message could still be presented with that vitality which attracts those who are seeking to know God.[44] Such renewal from within, of course, demands the confidence that, however small the movement – or however scattered its supporters – it has a treasure to offer which has sprung out of its own history. In an introduction to a book of Ethiopian illuminated manuscripts, by Jules Leroy, he points out that some of their religious paintings have a style, quality and beauty amazingly like those of eight-century Irish paintings: a strange coincidence, since artists in the two countries could never have met or exchanged those ideas which might have assisted these expressions of their religious beliefs.[45] May there not be, in areas of remote rural Methodism, resources which, from within, can be developed without those "injections of hope" which somehow some believe the wider Connexion should be giving? For isolated, rural religion does not *need* to deteriorate into mere defence against an alien world nor become the forerunner of a stagnation which that world will barely notice. It has so much potential in environments where order and permanence reveal God's creative activity and which are so much in contrast with the disorder and uncertainties of city life.

In April 1984, it was possible to return from South Warwickshire to Blinn'd Lonnin (Blind Lane), near Newlands, Drybeck, leave the car and walk straight to a holly bush with a blackbird nest in it and be able to show visitors from Sheffield the beauty and texture of one of the four eggs. Over forty years ago, the same sort of bush was used by the same sort of bird to lay the same sort of eggs to rear the same sort of family which would sing the same song. The fledgling from one of the 1984 eggs (as local ornithological history tends to show) would be eaten by a farm cat; another would die at the teeth of a stoat; another would die of cold and the fourth would live to sing its praises to its mate. So the strain would survive. The real problem however, would be at the edge of the nest, when the young birds would be most at risk – when the world, for a few brief moments, would be testing the faith and courage of both the new adventurers and the ageing parents – who would somehow imagine that they could both keep them at home and send them away at the same time.

Hear, then, the 'parable' of the blackbird in this other Eden. Methodism worships in almost precisely the same way as it has always worshipped. It uses the same, simple, sacred space. It hopes that if it rears its children as they were always reared, they will sing the same hymns Methodism used to sing. For a few of its children the hope is fulfilled. But the edge of the nest, though problem for the blackbird, is opportunity for the Methodist. Worms, insects, care and attention, lavished upon the young birds in the nest, are of no avail, nor ever can be, once the nest is left. But Baptism, teaching and nurture in the faith, add up to far more because this love may continue long after the Sunday School (that once-supposed nursery of the Church) has ceased to be a popular meeting-place for those young people who have begun to look elsewhere for their identity and their excitement. This love, this "life of God in the soul of man", is that which renews the holy Community and which may bring back into its fellowship those who, at Baptism, were first received. It is not the kind of love and concern which those without religious beliefs sometimes show but it springs from the faith which says "we love because He first loved us". It is this consequence of faith which prompts that unending care for young people (by individual, pastoral concern and in youth groups - large or small - of fellowship or community activity)[46] and which means, therefore, that our rural Methodism need not be in hopeless predicament. Though this other Eden may not be easily found on the tourist map or even on a map of world religions, neither negligence nor defeatism should be allowed to erode the vast potential of its beliefs.

---

1 *Methodist Recorder*, 1.7.1982, p. 18.
2 *Kirkby Stephen, Appleby, and Sedbergh Wesleyan Methodist Church Record* (December 1906), p. 3.
3 Exodus 16, verse 23.
4 Rufus M. Jones, *Studies in Mystical Region* (London, 1923), p. 459.
5 Kristensen, W. Brede, *The Meaning of Religion* (The Hague, 1960), p. 471.
6 John Wesley, *The Journal*, III, 328.
7 *Ibid.*, IV, 126.
8 *Ibid.*, V, 442.
9 *Ibid.*, VI, 54.
10 *Ibid.*, VI, 136.
11 *Ibid.*, VI, 342.
12 *The Methodist Hymn Book*, No. 956, verse 3.
13 *Kirkby Stephen, Appleby and Sedbergh Wesleyan Methodist Church Record* (December, 1906), p. 3.
14 *The Methodist Hymn Book*, No. 686, verse 4.
15 *Ibid.*, No. 386, verse 1.
16 *Ibid.*, No. 386, verse 4.
17 As in Psalm 84, verses 1-2 and 4-5.
18 *The Methodist Hymn Book*, No. 678, verses 1 and 2.

[19] *Kirkby Stephen, Appleby and Sedbergh Wesleyan Methodist Church Record* (December, 1906), p. 3.

[20] George Eayrs, "Developments, Institutions, Helpers, Oppostion" in W. J. Townsend, H. B. Workman and G. Eayrs, *A New History of Methodistm* (London, 1909), I, 288.

[21] *The Constitutional Practice and Discipline of the Methodist Church* (London, 1981), p. 63.

[22] *Ibid.*, p. 64.

[23] *Ibid.*, p. 63.

[24] 2 Samuel 6, verses 6 and 7.

[25] Matthew 6, verse 9.

[26] Romans 8, verse 16.

[27] Galations 5, verses 22-23.

[28] *Kirkby Stephen, Appleby and Sedbergh Wesleyan Methodist Church Record* (December, 1906), p. 3.

[29] *Cumberland and Westmorland Herald* (August-September, 1981).

[30] See pp. 10-13.

[31] In a letter to me, dated 1.2.1983.

[32] In a letter to me, dated 8.2.1983.

[33] In a letter to me, dated 22.2.1983.

[34] S. Nettleton, in *Primitive Methodist Magazine* (London, 1847), Obituary No. 23, p. 575.

[35] Minutes of the *Carlisle Wesleyan District Meeting, 1892.*

[36] James 4, verse 4.

[37] 1 Corinthians 5, verse 10.

[38] James 1, verse 27.

[39] John 1, verse 10.

[40] John 7, verse 7.

[41] *The Book of Offices* (London 1936), p. 102.

[42] *Methodist Recorder*, 1.7.1982, p. 18.

[43] *Methodist Hymn Book*, No. 473, verse 2.

[44] Bede Griffiths, *Return To The Centre* (Collins, Fount Paperbacks, 1978), pp. 117-118.

[45] Jules Leroy, *Ethiopia: Illuminated Manuscripts* (New York Graphic Society, by arrangement with UNESCO, Paris 1961), p. 13.

[46] The Reverend John E. Clarke (The Arthur Rank Centre, National Agricultural Centre, Stoneleigh, Kenilworth, Warwickshire), one of whose concerns is the small, rural Methodist Church, says that the Home Mission Division and the Division of Education and Youth (of the Methodist Church) are shortly making available material which will be useful to those who are involving themselves in work among young people.

BIBILIOGRAPHY

1. *Sources relating to the area of study.*
(a) Manuscript sources:

At the County Records Office, County Hall, Kendal:

Minutes of Kirkby Stephen and Appleby Wesleyan Circuit Local Preachers Meetings.

Minutes of Kirkby Stephen, Appleby and Sedbergh Wesleyan Circuit Local Preachers Meetings.

Minutes of Kirkby Stephen and Appleby Wesleyan Circuit Quarterly Meetings.

Minutes of Kirkby Stephen, Appleby and Sedbergh Wesleyan Circuit Quarterly Meetings.

Minutes of Gaisgill Wesleyan Trustees Meetings.

Minutes of Kirkby Stephen Wesleyan Trustees Meetings.

Minutes of Nateby Wesleyan Trustees Meetings.

Minutes of Brough Primitive Methodist Circuit Preachers Meetings.

Minutes of the Brough Branch of the Barnard Castle Primitive Methodist Circuit.

Minutes of Brough Primitive Methodist Circuit Quarterly Meetings.

Minutes of Appleby Wesleyan Methodist Association Circuit Quarterly Meetings.

Minutes of Appleby United Methodist Free Church Circuit Quarterly Meetings.

Minutes of Appleby United Methodist Circuit Quarterly Meetings.

Baptismal Register: Appleby Tabernacle United Methodist Free Church (1850-1932).

Baptismal Registers: Brough Primitive Methodist Circuit (1900-1960).

Circuit Schedule Book of the Kirkby Stephen and Appleby Wesleyan Circuit (June, 1932).

Special Schedule for 1881: United Methodist Free Church Societies.

Interments in the Wesleyan Methodist's Cemetery KIRKBY STEPHEN (24.5.1843-5.2.1900).

Register of the names of the Members of the Wesleyan Methodist Association in the Appleby Circuit, commencing in 1840. December 21st.

Report of the Brough Primitive Methodist Circuit to the Carlisle and Whitehaven District (1887).

Report of the Wesleyan Connexional Local Preachers Committee to the Manchester Conference (1918).

Brough Primitive Methodist Quarter-day account books (1851-1932).

Rules and Regulations relating to Local Preachers (printed, and bound into the Kirkby Stephen and Appleby Wesleyan Local Preachers Minute Book (1908-1924)).

At the John Rylands University Library of Manchester (The Methodist Archives):

Minutes of Whitehaven and Carlisle Wesleyan District Meetings (1801-1920).

Minutes of the Inghamites (1755-1760).

The Account Book of the Reverend William Harland, Primitive Methodist Travelling Preacher (1831-1842).

Pastoral Address to the Wesleyan Methodist Societies in the Appleby Circuit (1855).

Letter from the Reverend John Kilner to Mr. Love (19.5.1865).

At the County Archives, Durham:

Barnard Castle Branch and Kendal Mission Account (of the Hull Primitive Methodist Circuit: 1837).

The Quarter Day Account and Minute Book of Brough Branch of the Hull Primitive Methodist Circuit: 1841.

Minutes of Brough Primitive Methodist Circuit Quarterly Meetings.

Minutes of Barnard Castle Primitive Methodist Local Preachers Meetings.

Minutes of Barnard Castle Primitive Methodist Circuit Quarterly Meeting, Report to District, 1841.

Minutes of Barnard Castle Primitive Methodist Circuit Quarterly Meeting, 1842.

In the British Library, London:

Letter from Richard Burn to Charles Lyttleton, Bishop of Carlisle, in the Stowe Manuscript 754, folio 112 (2.8.1763).

In the effects of the late Miss M. K. Thompson, Long Marton:

Certificate of Long Marton Protestant Dissenters seeking registration of Edmund Thompson's house for public worhsip (28.12.1813).

Wesleyan Methodist Centenary Book, 1841.

In the possession of Mrs. D. Braithwaite, Kirkby Stephen:

Diary of John Parkin.

In the possesion of Mr. T. K. Clarke, Howgill Castle, Milburn:

Temperance League Certificate (framed original: May 1902).

The following Methodists (and others) have provided information:

Mrs. H. Alderson (Orton).
Mr. W. H. Alderson (Orton).
Mr. D. Capstick (Newbiggin-on-Lune).
Mr. T. Capstick (Kirkby Stephen).
Mr. S. Dent (Bolton).
Mrs. M. M. Ewin (Raisbeck).
Miss M. Harper (Kirkby Stephen).
Revd. E. D. Hodgkiss (Tebay).
Canon Markham (Morland Anglican).
Mrs. M. Metcalfe (Kirby Thore).
Mr. W. Robinson (Crosby Garrett).
Mr. J. Thornborrow (Tebay).
Revd. D. West (Kirkby Stephen Baptist).

Revd. G. K. Johnson (Superintendent of the Barnard Castle Circuit in 1977), who kindly allowed me to see the documents, listed above, before their deposit at the County Archives, Durham.

(b) *Printed* sources:

A Literary Antiquarian, *The Manners and Customs of Westmorland,* and the adjoining parts of Cumberland, Lancashire and Yorkshire, in the former part of the Eighteenth Century (Kendal, 1827).

BARBER, W. T. A., "The Work of British Societies, in W. J. TOWNSEND, H. B. WORKMAN and G. EAYRS, ed., *A New History of Methodism,* 2 vols. (London, 1909).

BOND, JOHN, *Golden Candlesticks, or sketches of the rise of some early Methodist Churches* (London, 1873).

BOUNDS, KENNETH, "From Lakes to Pennine Way", *Down To Earth* (The Methodist Home Mission Report, Westminster, 1980).

BRAITHWAITE, MATTHEW, *History of Wesleyan Methodism in the Bishop Auckland Circuit* (Bishop Auckland, 1885).

BRUNSKILL, STEPHEN, *The Life of Stephen Brunskill of Orton, 60 years a Wesleyan Methodist Local Preacher,* written by himself (London and Kendal, 1837).

BULMER, T. F., *History of Westmorland* (Manchester, 1885).

CLARKE, DAVID F., "Another 'Son to Susanna(h)' ", *Proceedings of the Wesley Historical Society* (Chester, December, 1972).

CLARKE, DAVID F., Benjamin Ingham (1712-1772), unpublished M.Phil. Thesis (Leeds University, 1971).

CLOSE, JOHN, *The Wise Man of Stainmore* (Kirkby Stephen, 1864).

DAVEY, CYRIL J., *The Methodist Story* (London, 1955).

EAYRS, GEORGE, "Developments, Institutions, Helpers, Opposition", in W. J. Townsend, H. B. Workman and G. Eayrs, ed. 2 vols. *A New History of Methodism* (London, 1909).

FERGUSON, R. S., *Early Cumberland and Westmorland Friends* (London, 1871).

FOX, GEORGE, Tercentenary edition, Norman Penney, ed., *The Journal of George Fox* (London, 1924).

GREGORY, J. R. and A. E., "Wesleyan Methodism - The Middle Period", in W. J. Townsend, H. B. Workman and G. Eayrs, ed., *A New History of Methodism*, 2 vols. (London, 1909).

HARRISON, A. W., BARBER, B. A., HORNBY, G. G. and DAVIES, E. T., *The Methodist Church. Its Origin, Divisions and Reunion* (London, 1932).

HAWKINS, JOSEPH, *O'er Hill and Dale and by the Solway Shore* (Watton, Norfolk, 1907).

JONES, RUFUS, M., "Seekers", in James Hastings, ed., *Encyclopaedia of Religion and Ethics*, 13 vols. (Edinburgh, 1920).

KENDALL, H. B., "The Primitive Methodist Church", in W. J. Townsend, H. B. Workman and G. Eayrs, ed., *A New History of Methodism*, 2 vols. (London, 1909).

MATTHEWS, CANON, and WHITEHEAD, JAMES F., *History of Appleby* (Appleby, without date).

MILLS, L. H. and GRAY, LOUIS, H., "Barsom", in James Hastings, ed., *Encyclopaedia of Religion and Ethics*, 13 vols. (Edinburgh, 1909).

NICHOLSON, J. W., *History of Crosby Garrett, Westmorland* (Kirkby Stephen, 1914).

NICHOLSON, JOSEPH, and BURN, RICHARD, *The History of Antiquities of the Counties of Westmorland and Cumberland*, 2 vols. (London, 1777).

PARROTT, F. W., *Vale of Eden Band of Hope Union 1873-1973* (Teesdale Mercury Ltd., Barnard Castle, 1973).

STEELE, A., *Life and Labours of Hodgson Casson* (London, 1854).

STEELE, ANTHONY, *History of Methodism in Barnard Castle and the Principal Places in the Dales Circuit* (London, 1857).

TYERMAN, L., *The Life and Times of the Rev. John Wesley, M.A.*, 3 vols. (London, 1878).

WATSON, JOHN K., "5 Days in May" in *Body and Soul* (Report of the Methodist Church Home Mission Division, London, 1983).

WESLEY, JOHN, *The Journal of the Rev. John Wesley, A.M.* Standard edition, 8 vols. (London, 1938).

WESLEY, JOHN, *The Letters of the Rev. John Wesley, A.M.*, 8 vols. (London, 1931).

WESLEY, JOHN, *The Works of the Rev. John Wesley, A.M.* 3rd edition, 14 vols. (London, 1831).

WHELLAN, WILLIAM, *History and Topography of Cumberland and Westmorland* (Pontefract, 1860).

WIDDUP, HENRY L., *Christianity in Cumbria* (Kendal, 1981).

At the County Record Office, County Hall, Kendal:
Circuit Plans:

Kirkby Stephen and Appleby Wesleyan (1881-1882).
Kirkby Stephen and Appleby Wesleyan (1882).
Kirkby Stephen and Appleby Wesleyan (1883).
Kirkby Stephen, Appleby and Sedbergh Wesleyan (1901-1902).
Kirkby Stephen, Appleby and Sedbergh Wesleyan (1902-1903).
Kirkby Stephen and Appleby Wesleyan (1920).
Brough Primitive Methodist (1922).
Kirkby Stephen and Appleby Wesleyan (1929).

At the John Rylands University Library of Manchester
(The Methodist Archives):

Aldersgate Primitive Methodist Magazine.
Primitive Methodist Magazine.
Wesleyan Methodist Magazine.
Methodist Recorder.

At the Herald Office, Penrith:

Cumberland and Westmorland Advertiser.

Mid-Cumberland and North Westmorland Herald.
Cumberland and Westmorland Herald.

In the care of the Reverend Albert W. Cornah, Superintendent of the Kirkby Stephen, Appleby and Tebay Circuit:

Kirkby Stephen, Appleby and Tebay Circuit Schedule (1976-1977).
Kirkby Stephen, Appleby and Tebay Circuit Plan (Oct.-Dec., 1982).

In the effects of the late Miss M. K. Thompson, Long Marton:

Appleby Wesleyan Circuit Plan: May-October, 1830.

Also:

Guild Syllabuses, Kirkby Thore (1934-1968), in the possession of Mrs. M. Metcalfe, Kirkby Thore.

Kirkby Stephen, Appleby and Sedbergh Circuit Magazine (Dec., 1905), in the possession of Mr. L. B. Harris, Winton.

Kirkby Stephen Appleby and Sedbergh Wesleyan Methodist Church Record (Dec., 1906), in the possession of Mr. L. B. Harris, Winton.

Crosby Garrett Methodist Chapel 1882-1982, a centenary celebration pamphlet by B. E. Umpleby.

Plan for the Westmorland Group of Baptist Churches (Oct.- Dec., 1982). In my own possession

Kirkby Stephen and Appleby Wesleyan Church Record (Nov., 1898).

Adult Collector's Book of the Methodist Missionary Society (1962-1966). In my own possession

Annual Report of the Free Church Federal Council (London, 1982).

Census Returns (1801, 1851 and 1971).

Lancaster Guardian (7.5.1971).

Ordnance Survey Map (Collins, Glasgow 1980).

Report of the Trustees for Methodist Church Purposes (Manchester, 1980).

Rules and Regulations for the Societies of the Primitive Methodist Connexion (M.R. Publishing, Leigh-on-Sea, 1975).

The Book of Offices being the Orders of Service authorized for use in the Methodist Church together with the Order for Morning Prayer (London, 1936).

The Constitutional Practice and Discipline of the Methodist Church (Methodist Publishing House, London, 1981).

The Methodist Hymn Book With Tunes (London, 1933).

The Scripture quotations in this publication are from the Revised Standard Version of the Bible, copyrighted 1971 and 1952 by the Division of Christian Education of the National Council of the Churches of Christ in the U.S.A.

2. *Secondary* sources:

BRAITHWAITE, W. C., *The Beginnings of Quakerism* (London, 1912).

COKE, DOCTOR and MR. MOORE, *The Life of the Reverend John Wesley, A.M.* (London, 1792).

COLWELL, JOHN, *Sketches of Village Methodism* (London, 1877).

DEFOE, DANIEL, *A Tour Thro' The Whole Island of Great Britain* (London, 1927).

ESKHOLME, GEORGE, *Sketch of the Life of Peter Eskholme of Summerbridge* (Bramley, 1885).

GRIFFITHS, BEDE, *Return To The Centre* (Collins, Fount Paperbacks, 1978).

JONES, RUFUS, M., *Studies in Mystical Religion* (London, 1923).

KRISTENSEN, W. BREDE, *The Meaning of Religion* (The Hague, 1960).

LEROY, JULES, *Ethiopia: Illuminated Manuscripts* (New York Graphic Society, by arrangement with UNESCO, Paris 1961).

PATTERSON, W. M., *Northern Primitive Methodism* (London, 1909).

RITSON, JOSEPH, *The Romance of Primitive Methodism* (London, 1909).

TAYLOR, E. E., *Friends Ancient and Modern Series,* No. 22 (London, without date).

TAYLOR, ROBERT, *The Hope of the Race* (London, 1946).

TELFORD, JOHN, *The Methodist Hymn-Book Illustrated* (London, 1906).

TYERMAN, L., *The Oxford Methodists* (London, 1873).

WESLEY, CHARLES, in OSBORN, G., ed., *The Poetical Works of John and Charles Wesley,* 13 vols. (London, 1872).

WILLIAMS, HENRY, W., *The Constitution and Policy of Wesleyan Methodism,* 2nd edition (London, 1882).

WORDSWORTH, WILLIAM, in HUTCHINSON, THOMAS, ed., *The Poetical Works of Wordsworth* (O.U.P., 1904).

INDEX

( ) denotes footnotes

Other references, especially to numerous place-names and a host of Methodist people can, alas, only be found by careful reading from cover to cover.